PICTURE
FRAMING
MADE EASY

PICTURE FRAMING MADE EASY

PENELOPE STOKES

Photographs by
Frank Ellis

BLANDFORD PRESS
LONDON

Blandford Press

an imprint of
Cassell plc
Artillery House, Artillery Row
London SW1P 1RT

First Published 1986
Reprinted 1987,1988

British Library Cataloguing in Publication Data

Stokes, Penelope
  Picture framing made easy.
  1. Picture frames and framing—Amateurs' manuals
  I. Title
  749'.7   N8550

ISBN 0 7137 1851 X

Distributed in the United States by
Sterling Publishing Co., Inc.,
2 Park Avenue, New York, NY 10016

Distributed in Australia by
Capricorn Link (Australia) Pty Ltd,
PO Box 665, Lane Cove, NSW 2066

Typeset by Word Perfect 99, Bournemouth

Printed in Great Britain by Richard Clay Ltd,
Chichester.

CONTENTS

INTRODUCTION

Mass-produced pictures are now widely and cheaply available. They are often sold already framed in somewhat unimaginative style to a rather low standard; this is almost inevitable when batches of dissimilar pictures are being framed on a production line at low cost. It usually comes as something of a shock to the buyer of an unframed reproduction, however, to find that the cost of bespoke framing may well exceed the price of the initial purchase. Much of this cost is labour and, with the trend toward doing it yourself, many people are considering framing their own pictures.

Cost savings may kindle your interest in home framing but further benefits will soon become apparent. Commercial framers may have the edge over the beginner in the speed with which they can turn out serviceable frames, but they do not offer the standard of finish that the enthusiast can apply to his or her own work. A hand-polished hardwood frame demonstrably outclasses the spray-coated products of commercial stock. Furthermore the home framer who opts to work in raw timber can choose from an enormous range of profiles to which any number of different finishes can be applied, but the commercial framer may only have two or three dozen mouldings, all of which are prefinished.

Doing it yourself therefore not only saves money but enables you to frame your pictures in distinctive and appropriate style to an above-average standard.

With increasing experience you can develop this interest into a paying hobby. There is more detailed advice to this end later in the book. Even in the early stages it is not an extravagant pastime. Most of the tools have practical uses round the house anyway. The materials tend to be reusable; the products of failure can often be recycled into the next attempt. You also have at your fingertips the facility to turn out inexpensive presents or unusual contributions to fund-raising sales, or simply to return favours.

You will be amazed at what issues from the attics of friends and family once your skill with the mitre saw becomes well known. In particular the closet artists will emerge in droves. There seems to be something other than expense which deters the amateur from taking his work to a professional for framing; a fellow amateur, equally fearful of criticism, is much more appealing.

You will soon find that 'pictures', even in the loosest sense of the word, hardly covers the range of subjects that you may want to frame. Needlework, collage, trophies and certificates may all benefit from some sort of framed enclosure to display and protect them.

Nonetheless this book begins at the beginning. The materials and techniques described presume little or no experience on the part of the reader and no unrealistic standards of workmanship; you will not be advised to throw away costly materials at the first blunder. Basic mistakes can be anticipated and avoided, but often they are not and remedies are at least as important as preventive measures. In short, this book is for the inveterate bungler.

1 · TYPES OF ART AND FRAME

Long before the advent of modern (detachable, glazed) frames, artists felt the need to surround their works with some sort of ornamental border. Medieval panel paintings (which were mainly ecclesiastical) usually incorporated a carved, raised edge to serve this purpose. In style these frames generally reflected the prevailing architectural forms and many looked very like doorways. Between the thirteenth and fifteenth centuries, however, artists began to use a separately constructed frame in carved and gilded wood. During the next two hundred years production of these separate frames passed from the artists themselves to the furniture craftsmen and by the seventeenth century they had become objects of elaborate workmanship, drawing their artistic inspiration from classical sources.

During the reign of Louis XIV all Europe looked to the court at Versailles for stylistic leadership and French designs prevailed, rather than the influences of the Italian artists who had dominated the Renaissance. These influences, however, did not penetrate the Low Countries where a stout and more severe tradition resisted French ostentation. Dutch frames of this period were designed to make greater use of the natural beauty of wood rather than lavish and intricate carving for their effect.

British tastes tended to veer between the two, according to the prevailing political climate.

Despite the modern preference for comparative simplicity the French-inspired frames of this period undoubtedly represented a peak of craftsmanship. But later in the eighteenth century the development of ornamental plasterwork rendered these woodcarving skills redundant and the foundations were laid for a truly awful era of frame embellishment which aimed to reproduce the French forms but failed dismally to match their standards of creativity. Many of these pretentious Victorian monstrosities are still around today, often adorning heavy portraiture in boardrooms and town halls. This is not to say, of course, that the Victorian period produced no frames of artistic merit but that they tended to be individual designs rather than the product of a dominant school.

Twentieth-century frames have become progressively plainer, rejecting the highly gilded and contoured surfaces of their

Fig. 1   Medieval panel frame.

Fig. 2   Renaissance frame.

Fig. 3   Louis XIV frame.

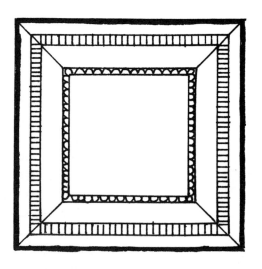

Fig. 4   Dutch seventeenth-century frame.

Fig. 5 Victorian frame.

predecessors. This trend has been taken to the ultimate by the 'no-frame' method which dispenses altogether with a surround; the art and glass are held together with metal clips.

FUNCTIONAL CONSIDERATIONS

It might be as well to pause here and consider that the purpose of the frame is not merely to enhance the appearance of the art. It has the much more practical function of protecting the work from the ravages of temperature change, humidity, chemical contamination, ingress of dust, fungus development and insect attack. This might sound like a rather alarming indictment of conditions in the average household but it is no exaggeration. Paper is an extraordinarily vulnerable substance: it readily absorbs atmospheric moisture which both deforms it and provides ideal conditions for mould growth. Silverfish (*Lepisma*) love to eat it. Ultraviolet light yellows it. Heat dries and embrittles it. Sulphur in the air turns to acid and stains it. In all, you might wonder why any artist with an eye to posterity paints on it.

Then again, many of the artist's media are delicate. Watercolours fade and inks are proverbially fugitive – in strong light they can vanish altogether with the passage of years. Unfixed pastel and charcoal can crumble and fall off the paper. Alternatively, if it is pressed hard against the glass and subjected to moisture or static build-up, the whole image can transfer from paper to glass (which can come as something of a shock to the person entrusted with re-framing).

The frame, then, must reconcile aesthetic demands with the needs of conservation. The basic wooden surround must hold glass, art and backing in a firm, sealed sandwich that will not loosen over the years to permit the ingress of enemies. There is, of course, an element of compromise if the art is of transient value. You may, for instance, decide to dispense with glass on a large poster because it is expensive and makes the whole picture unduly heavy. Alternatively you might decide that a modern print needs glass but should not be confined by a border, in which case you could select the 'no-frame' method described earlier. This can look very good on some pictures but offers no long-term protection because the sides of the sandwich are open.

CONVENTIONAL STYLES

With these practical considerations in mind you can now think about the stylistic element. There are no strict rules governing what is or is not good taste in framing, but there are some traditional practices which combine commonsense with a kind of aesthetic consensus. Do not feel bound by them if you feel strongly that your picture would look better treated differently. To live in harmony with what is on your walls you should not feel that your instinctive judgement has taken second place to some arbitrary canon of artistic fashion.

Fig. 6   Corner detail of a canvas stretcher.

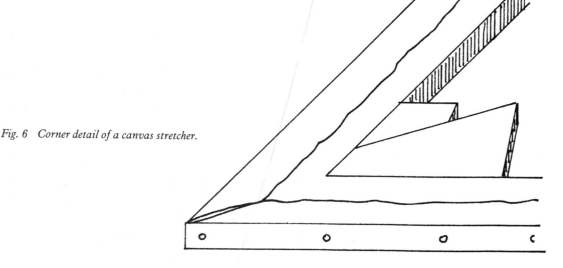

12

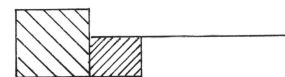

Fig. 7 Oil canvas in a baguette.

Oil paintings and acrylics are not glazed (except occasionally in museums for protection against vandalism) because they should already have been given a coat of protective varnish by the artist. They also need air circulating around them. Such pictures may be on a stretcher, which is a rectangular frame over which the canvas is nailed (Fig. 6). The corners incorporate wedges which can be tapped in harder to tauten the canvas (but beware of stretching old canvases – they can split unexpectedly). The wooden battens of the stretcher are usually too deep to be hidden by the side of the frame and project out slightly from the back. Most people consider that this is acceptable because it is not plainly visible from the front; if you want to avoid it you must choose a moulding with a deep rebate (see Chapter 4).

Some oils and acrylics are on canvas-covered board, which does not present problems of depth. Hard-up amateur painters often paint on hardboard. (Such is the force of their inspiration they rarely check first that the piece is a true rectangle, thus setting up problems for the framer.)

Conventional taste usually accords a wide moulding (at least 50 mm or 2 in) to oils. Some more modern works may need a defined edge but minimal visual distraction, and may be better suited by a baguette, which is a natural stripwood surround lapped rather than mitred at the corners (Fig. 7). A third option is a 'floating frame' whereby an outer frame embraces a black 'field' on which the canvas appears to 'float' (with or without an inner frame, depending on the state of the edges of the canvas). This is shown in Fig. 8.

Mounts (known in the USA as 'mats') are not used on oils or acrylics. If it is felt that some visual break is needed between the picture and its frame this can be achieved by the inclusion of a slip, or liner, which is a second, inner frame tucked under the lip of the outer frame. It is usually narrower than the outer frame and may be either gilded or linen-covered, or both.

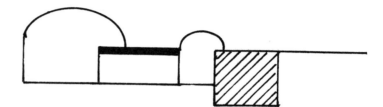

Fig. 8 Oil canvas in a floating frame.

Watercolours, being more delicate in nature and appearance, must not only be glazed but also spaced back from the glass to avoid damaging contact with condensation. This is normally done by the inclusion of a mount, which is a cardboard window separating the two (see Fig. 9).

In general small pictures look better in large mounts and vice versa. Watercolour mounts are usually neutral in colour: cream, beige, quiet greens, browns and greys. Beware of teaming a magnolia type of off-white with a picture that includes a lot of pure white; the mount will look grubby in contrast.

The surrounding frame on a watercolour is usually dark, plain and narrow.

Pastel, chalk and charcoal drawings should be sprayed with a fixative

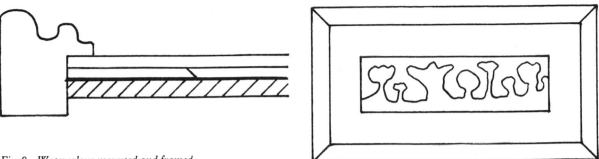

Fig. 9 Watercolour mounted and framed.

to prevent them literally falling off the paper. Even when fixed they need to be separated from the glass but a mount may not look right. In such cases you can use a fillet or spacer which is a very narrow strip of wood or card fixed inside the frame between glass and art (Fig. 10). It is not intended to be seen.

Print is a word loosely used to mean any reproduced art as opposed to a one-off original. In its strictest artistic sense, however, it refers to limited runs of copies produced under the artist's supervision. Traditional processes include wood and lino blocks, aquatint, mezzotint and lithography. Silk screen (serigraphy) is the modern method for short runs of bold, brightly-coloured imagery such as posters.

Prints are often signed by the artist and numbered, e.g. 15/350 at the bottom would indicate that this was the fifteenth impression from a run of 350. Theoretically the lower the number the more valuable the

Fig. 10 Frame with spacer (fillet).

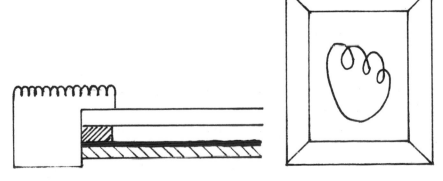

print since the plate becomes microscopically more worn with each impression. The first few run off will be marked 'A/P' in place of a number, meaning 'artist's proof'. There may also be insurance copies and exhibition copies in addition to the numbered total taken from the plate.

Prints produced by a plate process will have a visible indentation around them caused by the impression of the plate. This plate mark should remain visible when the print is mounted and framed since it is part of its authenticity. The same goes for any signature or number at the bottom.

Black and white etchings (produced by metal plate engraving), lithographs and suchlike were traditionally mounted only in white, ivory or cream. Purists would allow a coloured mount only on a coloured print. This principle is not rigorously observed nowadays.

Reproductions are distinct from prints, being mass-produced copies of old masters, popular modern paintings or even old prints. They are usually printed by photographically-based processes such as photogravure and photolithography and can be of very high quality in their fidelity of detail.

Unlike prints which are the same size as their originals reproductions are often smaller. Many 'art' greetings cards are mini-reproductions of quite reasonable quality and offer a good choice to the home framer wanting to fill walls on a low budget.

High-street picture shops now sell a large number of block-mounted reproductions of popular famous works. These are already varnished and ready to hang on the wall. If, however, you feel that the effect is somewhat bald, you can treat a block mounted work in the same way as an oil canvas (from which it may well have been taken in the first place). If you use the floating frame method you can dispense with the inner frame; the block can stand on a platform slightly proud of the fabric-covered background (see Fig. 11) bordered by a wooden frame. In this way the picture comes out boldly to meet the eye, which makes a change from the conventional arrangement whereby the eye is taken in to the picture.

In general, reproductions are probably best framed in the style appropriate to the original from which they were taken, allowing for the fact that, unless varnished, they will need to be glazed.

Paintings on wooden panels should be varnished for protection and then treated as oil canvases.

Photographs need to be kept away from contact with glass and are thus usually mounted. They also need to be stuck down to a backing

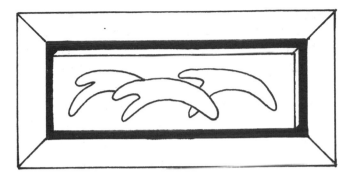

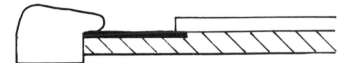

Fig. 11 *Block-mounted picture in a floating frame.*

card, being prone to curling, and this can be done either with a spray adhesive designed for the purpose or dry mounting tissue.

Posters and large screenprints present the framer with problems of size, weight and expense. Unless they are of long term interest it is perhaps best to dispense with glass and mount them onto something rigid like thick hardboard and then varnish them for protection. Acrylic glass-substitute (see Chapter 7) can be used; it is a good deal lighter (but no cheaper) than glass. Posters tend to look better without a surrounding conventional frame and therefore this acrylic sheet can be fixed by the 'no-frame' method described in Chapter 6.

Needlework such as tapestry and embroidery must first be stretched into shape and mounted onto a rigid backing. Glass will protect it from airborne dust and grime, but there is no doubt that fabric loses a lot of its textural impact behind glass so you must weigh the short and long term benefits. If glazed, needlework should be spaced from the glass with a fillet. If the edges are rough or unworked and you feel a surrounding mount is needed, then cover it with a material close to or compatible with the base material of the work.

Three-dimensional objects such as coins, medals, shells, fans or collage need a shadow box. This, as shown in Fig. 12, is a shallow display case made with a second, inner frame fitted under the glass to create depth. Even where this space is not strictly necessary (i.e. for a flat object) it lends a precious, cossetted look to the object on display.

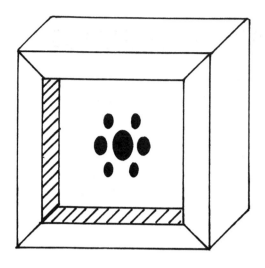 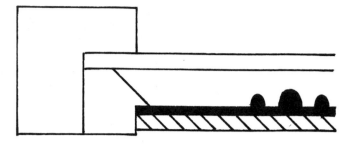

Fig. 12 Shadow box.

The objects are generally fixed to a fabric (e.g. velvet or linen) background as described in Chapter 3.

Leatherwork can be mounted onto a textured base and framed but should not be glazed because it needs to 'breathe'.

Stylistic guidelines such as these are given to assist rather than to dictate choice. The one constant rule for all work is that the frame is always the bridesmaid, never the bride. It should not be so eye-catching as to make one notice it before the picture. The purpose is to serve the art, perhaps to lend importance to it, to guide the eye into it and to assist in blending the work harmoniously into its surroundings.

If you yearn to produce extravagant, arresting frames with which no pictures can compete then put them around mirrors!

2 · GETTING STARTED

The first step in deciding to frame at home is to lay claim to your work area. For most people there will not be many options. A garage workshop where frames can be left undisturbed while adhesive or woodstain dry off is ideal but such conditions are not available to all. There are clean and dirty operations in framing and if they are not separated by space then they must be kept rigorously apart in time. Basically all operations carried out on the artwork itself (measuring, trimming, mounting) must be done on a clean surface with clean hands. The construction of the frame itself is dirty work involving sawdust, adhesive, filler, paint, stain and solvents. Never allow the artwork to come anywhere near this.

If one worktable is to serve both these purposes it would be best to have two interchangeable surfaces for clean and dirty work. If it also happens to be your kitchen table you would not, in any case, want it damaged by accidental spillages or scrapes. A large sheet of hardboard will be quite adequate if the table is smooth and level. If your table is wobbly it cannot be used for sawing. A portable workbench with movable 'jaws' comes in handy for this because you can clamp the mitring device into it. You can also, in good weather, take the whole operation outside and minimise domestic disruption.

You will need a fair amount of space around you to manipulate lengths of moulding which tend to be about 2.5 m (8 ft) long. If you have to work in restricted space your supplier may be able to cut the moulding up for you into manageable lengths.

Good light is needed in the framing area. If natural light is insufficient make sure that you are not working in your own shadow from overhead light. An anglepoise-type light clamped to the edge of the table can be helpful. Some crucial operations are best done in daylight, notably colour matching of mounts to art and the inspection of glass before fitting it into the frame. What seems like a perfectly clean piece of glass in artificial light develops a mysterious peppering of dust overnight, plainly visible in the cold light of the morning. This is particularly annoying if you have sealed it into the frame.

Ventilation should also be taken into account because you will be using solvents which must evaporate freely. Temperature should not be much below 15°C (approximately 60°F), not so much for the comfort of the framer but because adhesives, polish and varnish do not perform well below this temperature.

PREPARING THE ARTWORK

First Aid

Very few pictures arrive at the framer's in pristine condition. Even relatively new reproductions have often been badly rolled. The nature of the framing decision is that pictures tend to wait around until their owners have some spare cash and that waiting time is rarely spent in ideal conditions.

Some damage is irremediable but there are a number of processes which can ameliorate the ravages of time and bad handling. It should be remembered that they all carry an element of risk and should be tried out on an unobtrusive corner of the art to test for unexpected reactions of the paper.

Creases can be made less noticeable with gentle pressing using a cool, dry iron through brown paper. Pressing will not smooth out buckling due to atmospheric distortion, i.e. where the picture has, in the past, been taped on all four corners and allowed to absorb moisture; nor can it hide the cracks that appear in heavily coated paper when it has been creased. However, it brings a measure of improvement to many pictures. Leave the picture weighted flat for some time afterwards.

General dirt can be taken off by gentle use of a soft gum eraser (beware of taking off part of a drawing). In the absence of this a piece of stale bread can be quite as effective.

Mildew is a spotty surface mould brought on by damp conditions. It should be possible to brush it off in a dry atmosphere. Failing that, scrape exceedingly carefully with the point of a sharp blade.

Foxing describes the brown discolourations that appear on old paper. They indicate the presence of fungus and will spread if not treated. A weak solution of mild bleach or feeding bottle steriliser (made up according to the bottle instructions) can be used with a paintbrush for spot treatment. Support the treated area as it becomes wet, and back it with absorbent paper. Keep well away from areas of the picture which may not be colour fast. When the mark has faded follow up with clean, cold water to rinse out the bleach or it will continue to eat into the fibres of the paper. Blot dry and leave flat.

Dull photographs can be brightened up by polishing with a good beeswax furniture polish. The same treatment can be applied to a varnished or laminated block-mounted picture.

Dull oil paintings may also benefit from polishing. If it fails to have much effect try a proprietary varnish cleaner from an art shop, but be aware that you are approaching the territory of the professional. Vigorous use of solvents can clean the entire painting out of existence. If the varnish cleaner does not do the job then the varnish itself is discoloured and needs to be taken off; this is not a job for the amateur.

Grease spots on paper should initially be attacked with an iron and blotting paper. If this does not work proceed to stronger measures (i.e solvents) with caution. A wad damped with dry cleaning fluid (carbon tetrachloride) or white spirit should help, but test in a corner first to make sure that it does not leave a tidemark.

Tears in paper should be mended from behind, ideally with Japanese tissue paper and starch paste. Stamp hinges will do for small tears. Ordinary adhesive tape will not do because it discolours and dries in time. There is however a new product which is designed for document repair and claims to have overcome the shortcomings of conventional plastic tapes.

Touching up is most definitely not recommended in most cases, but there are a few occasions when the picture is not valuable or original (or someone else's property) when a scratch or scuff through to the white centre of the paper will tempt you. A very light brush with the appropriate watercolour from a paintbox is the best medium. The difference in texture will be evident but may be less obtrusive than the original damage. The inherent danger in this operation is over-enthusiasm. With paintbox and brush to hand you start looking for more opportunities and suddenly find you have gone too far.

Pastels, charcoals and chalk drawings have loose-textured surfaces which should be fixed before framing to prevent particles from dropping down inside the frame. A squirt of hair lacquer will do for pictures of insignificant financial or sentimental value but you should use the proper product from an art shop for anything of lasting worth.

Having cleaned your picture, protect it until it is ready to go into the frame. Transparent plastic document sleeves are ideal because they are strong but permit you to take measurements, try samples, show the picture to your friends etc without continual handling of the paper. Unfortunately they are not easily obtainable in large sizes. Transparent film offers a lesser degree of protection but tends not to stay in place unless the picture is rigidly backed. It is often a good idea to cut the backing board at this stage and to use this as your template for frame size checking, glass cutting etc so that the picture can be put safely away in some flat place. Picture-framing gremlins are uncommonly skilful at transferring dollops of indelible liquid onto unprotected pictures, particularly those that belong to someone else!

Squaring and Measuring

Modern prints and reproductions are nearly always accurately squared, being machine products, but originals and old prints are often out of true. The quickest way to check is with a setsquare in three corners (the fourth must of course be 90 degrees if the others are). It is not sufficient simply to check that the diagonals are equal, as some authorities recommend because, as Fig. 13 shows in exaggeration, it is perfectly possible to have equal diagonals on an irregular quadrilateral.

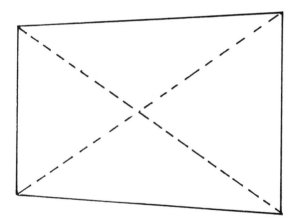

Fig. 13   Equal diagonals on an irregular quadrilateral.

If your picture is out of true you have the choice of bringing the frame (or mount) in to a trimmed (or folded) regular shape, or to take the frame (mount) outwards to create a border around the picture. This latter is preferable if the picture is valuable or carries a plate line, title or signature. If there is insufficient paper surplus extending beyond the image area then the picture can be laid onto a background sheet (see 'drop-on mounts' in the next chapter) and this used to create the border.

Having confirmed the angles of the corners, now prepare to measure the sides. In view of the accuracy to which you will have to work there is much to be said for going metric and working to a tolerance of 1 millimetre and thus whole numbers. In imperial units you will have to work, in some cases, to $1/16$ or even $1/32$ of an inch, and when you come to add on mount widths, moulding mitre allowances and so on

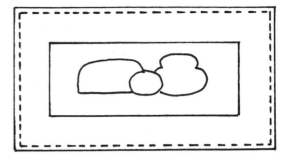

Fig. 14 Sight and rebated sizes.

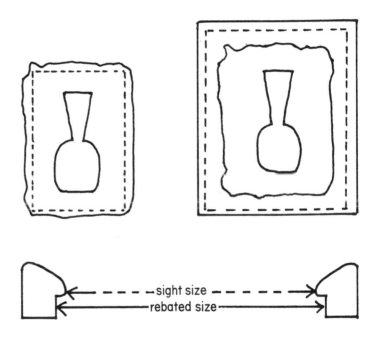

you will be very prone to error juggling these fractions.

Determine first the sight or view size, that is the area which you wish to see inside the confines of the mount or frame. It may be slightly larger than the actual image area if you are including a self-border, or slightly smaller if you want to hide a damaged or unfinished edge.

Get into the habit of quoting your measurements (even to yourself) consistently. Vertical × horizontal is the current practice in the UK art world; in the USA the reverse is normal, i.e. horizontal × vertical. Either way consistency is to be preferred or you will one day make a blunder with a mount whose margins are not uniform. It is also

23

Fig. 15   Portrait and landscape proportions.

common to describe pictures (for the purpose of framing) as either 'portrait' or 'landscape', which has no bearing on the subject of the imagery but defines vertical and horizontal rectangles respectively (Fig. 15).

This sight size is your initial working dimension. The rebated size (the size of the contents of the frame) is slightly larger because it takes into account that small border which disappears under the lip of the frame.

3 · MOUNTS (MATS)

Most glazed pictures need a mount, or mat, for conservation reasons. The paper is held back from the glass and thus protected from moisture which may collect in minute but damaging quantities on the inside of the glass. However, most people, when choosing a frame, decide upon a mount for aesthetic reasons. There is often a requirement for a visual 'breathing space' between the picture and its frame. Pictures whose edges lead directly into a solid border often look cramped and there is nothing so uncomfortable on the eye as a wall full of pictures trying to escape from their frames.

Pictures which do not merit long term conservation can be mounted by the 'drop-on' method, i.e they are fixed onto a background of card or paper (Fig. 16a). This can fulfil the aesthetic requirement but does not protect the art from glass contact in the way that a window mount

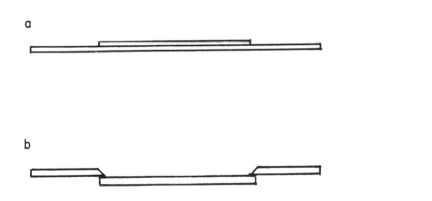

Fig. 16 Drop-on mount (a), window mount (b), and a combination of the two (c).

does. A window mount is cut from mountboard consisting of layers of white card faced with a top layer of colour. Thus the cut edge of the window (which is usually bevelled to an angle of 45 degrees) shows as a white outline. One millimetre of thickness is sufficient to hold the art back from condensation which may form on the glass (Fig. 16b).

You might want to show the edges of your artwork. Handmade paper has a wavy edge (known as the deckle) intended for display. Postage stamps, old documents with missing corners and suchlike should not be tucked under the edge of a window mount so the solution is to use both methods and allow the drop-on mount to show as a narrow border within the window (Fig. 16c).

COLOURS

The mount must not conflict or compete with the picture. Usually the safest course is to pick a colour which matches with some artistic detail rather than a dominant colour from the picture, which may risk diluting the impact of the work itself. If an exact match is wrong or difficult, try tints, shades or tones derived from colours in the picture. (A tint is a base colour modified by the addition of white, a shade the base colour plus black, and a tone the base colour with additions of both black and white.) If you think that any sort of attempt at tonal matching is wrong, try colours which are in the same mood as the subject matter. Warm colours are better for living subjects, cooler ones for abstracts. Earth colours suit landscapes; blues and greys suit seascapes. Strong colours are best reserved for robust pictorial imagery (which need not itself be in bright colours); they cannot be used successfully to strengthen a shy picture.

It is of course essential to try colour swatches (preferably as corner-shaped samples) against the picture in good light and to rely ultimately on your own judgement.

SIZES AND PROPORTIONS

This is a question upon which to dither almost interminably. It will be influenced by the following.

1) The size of the picture. Small pictures command more attention in large mounts, whereas in a narrow mount they can look lost and insignificant. Large pictures tend to have small mounts for reasons of practical accommodation.

2) The moulding to be used to make the frame. You may not yet have made this decision, but bear in mind that you will not want either one to duplicate the width of the other. The result is a stripey effect which diverts the eye from the picture. To be safe ensure that your mount is not less than twice the width of the moulding (or not more than half, if you are using a narrow mount with a wide moulding).

3) Any existing border or margin around the picture. This may be a printed one that you wish to show or perhaps the allowance needed to show a title or signature at the bottom. Such allowances usually look best running the whole way around the picture.

4) The wall space available. This should not override artistic imperatives but may well be a factor in finding a home for a large picture in a small house!

It used to be the rule that the bottom margin of the mount should be wider than the top and side margins to allow for the optical foreshortening effect of pictures hung above eye level. Nowadays it is not quite so common; ceilings are lower and picture levels have descended with them. Also the mass production of mounts is more economical if the margins are uniform!

Nonetheless a picture can often seem slumped in its frame if the mount margins are the same all the way round. You can increase the base by as little as 10 per cent and counteract this fact without creating any obvious visual discrepancy. Alternatively you can opt for a much larger increase, say 20 or 25 per cent, with the intention of making the thickened base a definite feature. Fig. 17 shows the effect of these variations. The same principle is often employed in the page layout of books.

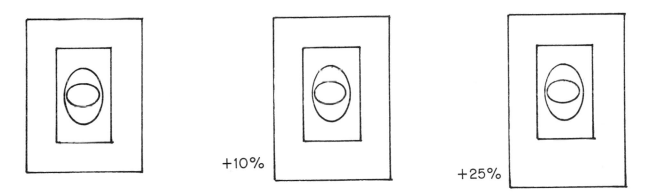

Fig. 17 Mounts with differing base sizes.

Elongated rectangles are usually exempt from this practice; they look better with equal margins all round.

Pictures that are nearly but not quite square can be converted to definite squares or definite rectangles by using differential margin widths on the mount.

Small pictures in series, e.g. stamps and cigarette cards, can be collected in one frame with a multiple aperture mount. This can be tricky to cut. It is better to plot your layout on to a sheet of squared paper first and be absolutely certain that your arrangement will look right. Cutting the apertures is hard enough without finding at the end of perfect handiwork that your geometry was faulty. In general the main, outer margin should be wider than the borders within the grouping. If the thought of achieving so many perfect corners appals you, you can get almost as good an effect by arranging them on a drop-on mount and then applying a window mount with one big aperture.

There may be other reasons for adjusting mount margins such as the need to make a picture fit an existing frame of different proportions. You have more flexibility with top and bottom than you do with side margins but you will find, after experiment, that in practice your options are as follows:

1) uniform width all round;
2) uniform top and sides, bottom a little or a lot wider;
3) uniform sides, top a little wider, bottom wider still; these narrow sides emphasise perpendicularity.

The other permutations, e.g. sides wider than base, do not generally please the eye.

There is a school of thought that prescribes an 'ideal rectangle' whose proportions derive from the 'golden ratio' favoured by classical mathematicians and architects. The theory is that the rectangle most visually acceptable has sides in the ratio 1:1.62 (Fig. 18). Many of the old Imperial paper sizes corresponded to this formula. The standard

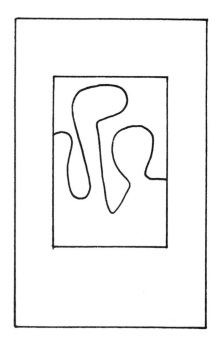

Fig. 18 Use of differential mount margins to convert a picture to a 'perfect rectangle'.

photographic enlargement ($3\frac{1}{2} \times 5\frac{1}{2}$ in) was also a close match until it was replaced by larger sizes which maintained a 2 in differential (4×6 in, 5×7 in, 8×10 in etc). You hardly need to be Euclid to see that one negative cannot be enlarged through this range of sizes without being subject to arbitrary cropping. Nonetheless the 2 in differential is now commonplace not only for photoprocessing but also for large-quantity, low-cost reproductions with dimensions under 12 in.

MAKING A DROP-ON MOUNT

These are a softer option; they are easier to make accurately and they are cheaper because you can use any good quality cover paper (but remember they offer no long-term protection to the artwork). The Ingres and Canson ranges stocked by most art shops have a good range of colours. Apsley card, which is heavier and comes in a less subtle colour range is also stocked by office stationers. Sugar paper, the cheapest of all, should be avoided because it fades very quickly. Embossed, marbled and handmade papers can make interesting mounts but they are not easy to obtain outside London.

'Wet mounting' was the old technique of laying pictures down onto backing paper. This involved pasting the entire back area of the picture and sticking it down to exclude air bubbles and creases. It was extremely hazardous, in that if it was messed up the picture would suffer irremediable damage. If the picture is very thin, absorbent or otherwise delicate then such pasting should be done onto the mount, taking care not to run onto what will be the margin area, if such is to be shown. Water-based starch pastes, such as those used for wallpaper, are the usual medium for this process.

Nowadays it is easier to use a purpose-designed spray adhesive from art shops. Whichever method you use you will need to countermount, i.e. to stick a sheet of brown paper to the back of the mount to stop it bowing as it dries. When the operation has been successfully completed the mounted art should be put between sheets of clean white blotting paper under weights to dry. If you do a lot of this it is handy to keep a few clean bricks for the purpose.

Wet pasting does not work on photographic paper, so either spray adhesive is used or dry mounting, i.e. the paper is bonded to the mount by a film of heat-activated (thermosetting) adhesive. Your local photographic or copy shop will do this fairly cheaply or you can have a go yourself using dry-mounting tissue from an art shop and a domestic iron.

Sticking the entire picture to a backing of heavy paper or card certainly helps to prevent the wrinkling and buckling that can occur in even the best of frames. However, it should never be done on art of any value, not only because of the risks involved in carrying it out but because art that has been irrevocably processed in any way loses its value. The acceptable alternative is 'tipping' which means lightly fixing the top corners to the mount. A tiny dab of glue is often used but it is better to make a tiny hinge out of gum strip. Stamp hinges are handy for small pictures. Avoid ordinary or double-sided transparent film tape; the adhesive is solvent-based and will eventually stain the paper.

Resist also the temptation to tape all four corners. The paper must be free to expand and contract with atmospheric changes within the frame, and if you pin its corners it will bulge outwards rather than stretch downwards. The results can never be successfully flattened out.

Whatever drop-on method you use, fix your picture to the backing before trimming to the finished size. It is much easier to measure margins out from the corners of the picture than to place it in an exact position on a precut sheet. (You may opt for flush mounting, i.e. trimming the mount to the same size as the picture, if it is being done solely for rigidity, in which case it does not matter.)

MAKING A WINDOW MOUNT

Mountboard for window mounts is available as 4-sheet or 6-sheet from art shops. 12-sheet is also obtainable but in a much reduced range of colours. It is not easy to cut and is best avoided by novices unless it is to be fabric covered. 4-sheet is the cheapest and easiest on which to experiment. Standard board size is approximately 22 × 32 in. 'Elephant' board is twice this size but colour choice is more restricted.

If you are framing something really valuable this sort of standard mountboard is not good enough because it contains acid traces which will ultimately attack the paper and stain it. You must use acid-free board, otherwise known as all-rag, conservation or museum board. It may have to be specially ordered through your art shop. The colour range is very limited, it is harder to cut than ordinary mountboard and, needless to say, considerably more expensive.

Window mount cutting is one of the most challenging tasks facing the home framer. It is essential that it is done well because a bodged mount looks awful no matter how well framed. The only remedy is to fabric cover it, but this is unlikely to be a happy solution if you did not think that a fabric-covered mount would suit your picture in the first place. Better to practise at some length and decide what your limitations are. If your results are utterly hopeless a professional framer might be prepared to mount the picture for you to frame subsequently. Or you could dispense with conventional mountboard and use instead something thinner and easier to handle like card; it will be much easier to cut but you will lose the smart bevelled edge and of course the protection because card is not thick enough to hold the picture back from the glass. You might feel that you could tackle 4-sheet mountboard but not attempt the bevel edge. If so, do not progress beyond the 4-sheet thickness; in thicker boards a vertical cut drops down to the picture rather abruptly.

Fig. 19 Tools for window mount cutting.

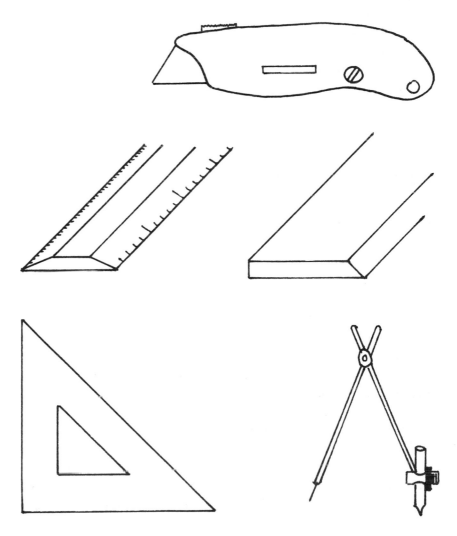

Professional framers cut window mounts with a long benchtop gadget with a fixed steel straightedge. The cutter assembly which slides along it has two blades; one is fixed to cut vertically and the other is fixed at 45 degrees. The home framer does his or her best with a utility knife, a ruler and a setsquare. If you can obtain a proper steel straightedge which has a bevelled edge you will find it much easier to work with. A pair of compasses comes in handy but is not essential.

Purpose-designed, hand-held mount cutters are available from art shops but are not cheap. If you are unable to try one out first and establish that it is of real assistance you might be better advised to spend your money on a straightedge which will certainly help in both glass and mount cutting.

Treat your mountboard as carefully as you would treat your picture; it marks easily and obviously. Make sure that your hands and equipment are clean (wipe the ruler and blade over with white spirit if they are likely to be greasy, and allow them to dry). Check also that your work surface is clean because you will mark and cut the board face down. If you do make the odd greasy fingermark you should be able to lift it by dabbing with white spirit which should dry without a tidemark, as should any accidental splashes of clean water.

Always mark and cut on the back of the mountboard; erased pencil marks and general abrasion from hand and ruler will show on the front surface.

Measure your picture and determine the sight size as described in the last chapter. The sight size must be a little smaller than the paper size or the bottom corners will literally fall through the window (unless your picture is already laid down onto an oversized drop-on mount).

Add to your sight size dimensions the mount margin width × 2 (allowing for any extra depth on the base, if applicable). Mark out this rectangle on the back of your mountboard. (Trust nobody: check first that all corners are right angles!) Cut out this rectangle making a vertical cut along your ruler or straightedge. Check the angles again.

Marking out the window can be done in several ways as shown in Fig. 20 and described below.

1) If you have a good quality pair of compasses lock them open to the desired margin width. Holding the apex in thumb and first two fingers of the hand draw the point down the outside edge of the board so that the pencil draws a parallel margin line on the board (Fig. 20a).

Fig. 20   Three methods of marking
out a mount.

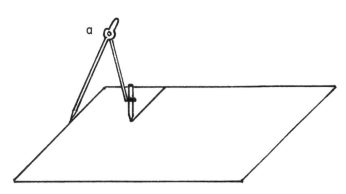

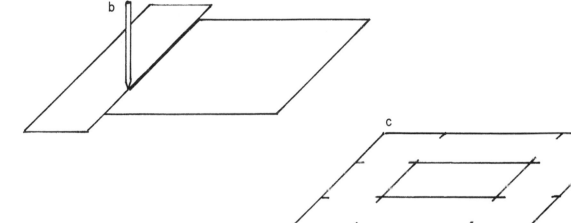

2) Cut a strip of spare mountboard to the exact margin width and use
    this as a template to mark the board. (But do not try to cut against
    it!) It is not quite as accurate as the method below but it does save
    time if you have several uniform mounts to cut (Fig. 20b).
3) The longer but safer way is to measure in from each corner and
    mark with a pencil. Join up opposite marks and then check the
    angles of your drawn window with a setsquare (Fig. 20c).

Whichever method is used make sure that your pencil is sharp and that
you use your ruler accurately; always read from directly above it,
never from a sideways angle. Slips of as little as 2 mm will be
noticeable in the frame.

    Now you are ready to cut. Use a piece of waste board under your
cutting line to stop the blade going through to the table; not only is it

bad for the table but it also quickly blunts the blade. Renew the blade whenever it becomes anything less than razor sharp (keep reject blades for less critical work such as cutting backing board). Hold the straightedge with one hand, and with the other draw the knife towards yourself steadily and firmly. Aim to complete the cut in one pass, i.e. stop neither halfway along the line, nor halfway into the depth of the mountboard.

If you are cutting a bevel by hand do not try to hold to the 45 degree angle of your straightedge; this will not be comfortable. 60 degrees looks just as good and is much easier (Fig. 21). Remember that a bevel cut means a deeper cut and therefore needs more pressure.

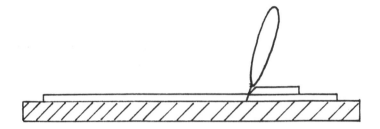

Fig. 21   Hand cutting a bevel.

You will need to overpass your corners by 3 mm (⅛ in) on a bevel cut in order to join up the corners on the face. Apart from this, try to avoid overcutting as it is fairly obvious on the face and looks slipshod.

If the centre waste does not drop out when all four cuts have been made turn it over to find out why. It may just be caught at the corners, in which case use the tip of the blade from the front to release them. If you try to force it through, your corners will be ragged.

Any slight roughness along the sides can be smoothed with very gentle strokes of the finest sandpaper, following the direction of the paper fibres. Too much roughness indicates either that your blade is blunt or that the scrap board underneath has become heavily grooved and must be changed.

When you have acquired some confidence on corners you might like to try rounded ones using a small gouge as a template.

If the picture is not to be framed immediately keep the waste to fit back in the space and protect the mounted picture.

FIXING THE PICTURE INTO THE MOUNT

This can be done in one of two ways.

1) The picture can be taped onto the back of the mount. Single tabs of masking tape or gumstrip on the top corner will suffice. Do not use transparent tape which discolours, dries out and drops off. Do not use double-sided tape which would make it impossible for the picture to be demounted without damage at a later date. Do not tape any more than the top two corners or the picture will buckle.

2) An altogether better solution is to make a hinged backsheet with a sheet of white card, cut to the same size as the mount. Tape it to the top of the mount with a hinge of masking tape running along most of the top edge. Then tip the picture in place on this backing (Fig. 22).

If the picture is on paper that is larger than the mount think twice before you trim it; it would certainly reduce the value of any serious work of art. It is better to fold the edges over.

Fig. 22 Fixing the picture into a mount.

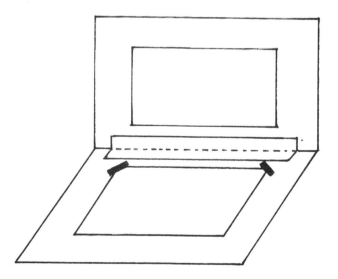

WASHLINES

Washlines are pen-and-ink or pencil lines drawn around the mount opening to create what is known as a French mount. Sometimes the space between them is filled with a light watercolour wash. There may be several lines with varying spaces between them. However, their purpose is to enhance rather than distract from the picture and for this reason they are normally confined to a fairly narrow band around the window extending no more than about 15% across the width of the mount. Examples of overexuberance in drawing washlines are not uncommon, usually to the detriment of the overall appearance of the picture.

The traditional instrument to use is a ruling pen which consists of a two-pointed nib which can be widened or narrowed with a screw. However, the hazards of dipping in and out of bottled ink are no longer necessary now that you can easily buy fibre tip pens of excellent (draughtsman) quality. Only the best will do, though, or you will get furry edges to your lines and blobs in the corners.

Colours are normally restrained but gold and silver are often effective in the right context. A well sharpened pencil or crayon looks good, particularly if the picture is in like media.

Do not mark your washline corners in pencil on the mount or you

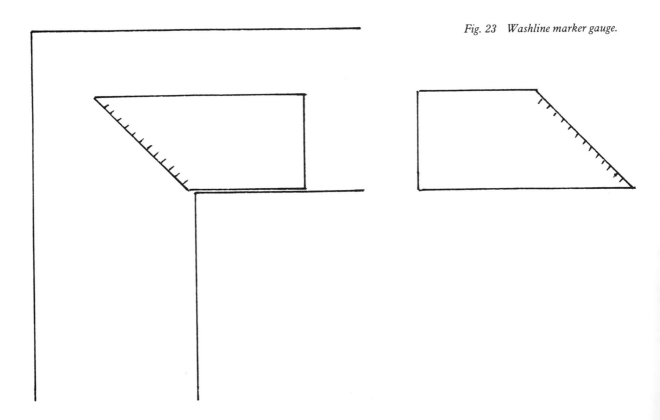

Fig. 23   Washline marker gauge.

will damage the mount surface when you rub them out. Use a pin to make tiny pricks. The easiest way to locate these marks is to make and use a washline marker gauge (shown in Fig. 23) as follows.

Cut out a piece of scrap card shaped as illustrated. The size is not important but the geometry must be precise. Mark with a fine fibre tip along the hypotenuse at, say, 2 mm intervals. Place this gauge on the corners of your mount and prick out your guide points as required. Then draw your lines joining these dots.

TITLE WINDOWS

A title window is a second aperture in the mount to show a title or signature which is placed too far below the picture to be included in the main window (Fig. 24). It is usually centred even if the inscription itself is not.

There is no special problem in cutting a title window other than the requirement for a little extra care in planning and marking out the margins. It would look wrong to insert a title window in the base of a mount as an afterthought; extra depth must be allowed to take it.

Fig. 24 Mount with a title window.

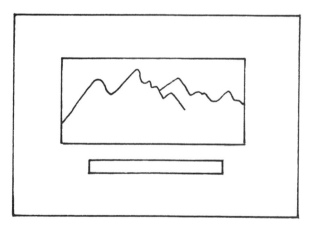

OVAL AND CIRCULAR MOUNTS

Oval and circular mounts are particularly suitable for portraits and flowers. They do not necessarily have to go into oval or circular frames.

Both types are most easily cut from a template which, in the case of circles, is not usually difficult to find in the kitchen. Ovals can be more of a problem; not only do they vary in area size but also in vertical/horizontal proportions.

Two methods of drawing ovals are detailed below.

1) Decide upon your desired height and width and draw a cross to these dimensions. Use a pair of compasses locked to a radius equal to half the long axis. Place the point on A and mark points B and C where the arc intersects the long axis (Fig. 25a). Then fix a drawing pin or tack firmly in each of B and C and around them knot a loop of non-stretch thread (such as carpet or linen thread) whose length is exactly ABC. Place your pencil in this loop and keeping it taut you will be able to draw your oval (Fig. 25b).

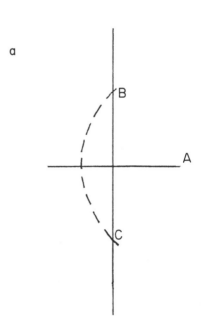

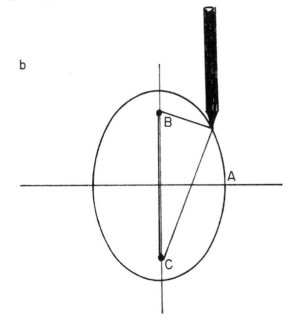

2) If you have an existing oval frame from which you would like to cut, say a 25 mm (1 in) wide mount, the method is slightly easier. Place the frame face-up on the back of the sheet and draw an outline of the rebated (rabbeted) size. For this you will need to poke your pencil under the lip of the frame so it helps to have a thin, well-sharpened pencil (see Fig. 26a). Then attach to your pencil a piece of dowel whose diameter, plus the diameter of your pencil, plus the width of the lip, equals the desired 25 mm. Run this dowel plus pencil around the lip of the frame (this time you

Fig. 25 How to draw an oval with string and pins.

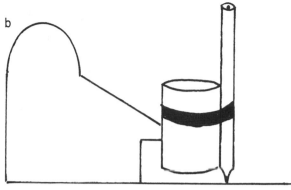

Fig. 26   How to draw an oval within a frame: a) same size; b) smaller than the frame.

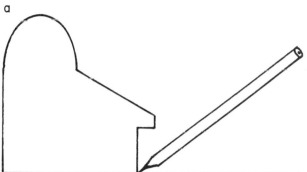

hold it exactly upright) making sure the frame moves not one jot from its original position. Thus you describe the inner oval (Fig. 26b).

If your oval is the aperture shape within a rectangular outer shape, mark these outer dimensions before you cut the inner oval, but do not actually cut them. It is easier to measure and mark out from a centre before the waste is removed. If, however, you cut the outside rectangle and then make a mess of cutting your oval you stand to waste more mountboard than is necessary.

Drawing the oval is only half the battle; you now have to cut it freehand. It is better not to attempt a bevel until you are very confident. For this reason it is better to use board no thicker than 4-sheet. In fact early efforts will probably be much more rewarding in card. It may help to cut twice − the first time lightly to make a track for the second, firmer cut. If your first cut strays off the line it should not have marked the face of the board.

If you are desperate you might resort to a pair of curved-blade scissors. Very fine sandpaper will help to smooth away your mishaps at the end.

DOUBLE MOUNTS

These are used to give the picture an extra border, usually dark and narrow, inside the main mount. The double bevel gives a more dramatic stepped effect than the use of a drop-on mount border within the window. A double mount also increases the height of the glass above the window and might be considered for a picture with a surface slightly in relief.

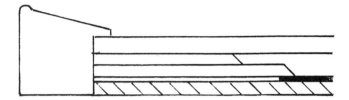

Fig. 27   Cross-section of a double mount.

The safest way to cut a double mount without messing it up is to treat the two mounts as entirely separate operations and not be tempted by slick methods of cutting both at once. It will be easier to line them up if both inner and outer mounts are cut to the same outer dimensions, although this is not strictly necessary.

First cut your inner mount to fit the sight size of the picture embracing both inner and outer margin sizes. Then measure a new sight size on the basis of this mount (Fig. 28a). Your outer mount can now be cut to this new sight size (Fig. 28b). Use double-sided tape to fix the two mounts together − a strip along each side − taking care to position them exactly (Fig. 28c). Then you can fix the picture into this double window exactly as if it were a single one (Fig. 28d).

FABRIC-COVERED MOUNTS

Fabric-covered mountboard is not easily obtainable through art shops, although it is sometimes used in the trade. Bevel cuts on prelaminated fabric board will show the white card interior whereas a home fabric mount is cut first and covered afterwards so the bevel is hidden. It is a handy way of hiding mountcutting blunders.

Silk and linen are traditional materials for fine subjects, hessian or burlap for more rugged mounts. Any fibre is worth experimenting with, but if it is of synthetic origin you should test a scrap piece with the adhesive you intend to use.

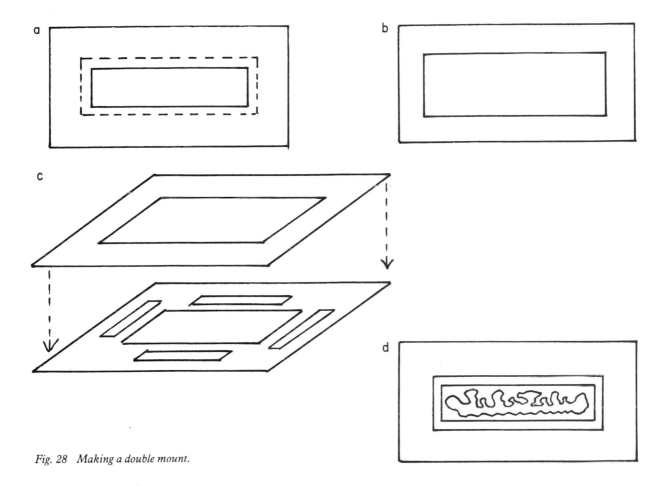

Fig. 28 Making a double mount.

Cut your mountboard as described earlier in this chapter. Bear in mind that the thickness of the fabric folding over the edge will contribute slightly to reducing the aperture size. Cut a rectangle of fabric (the weave should run horizontally) about 25 mm (1 in) larger all round than your mount. Paste or spray your mount face (including the bevelled edge) with adhesive and press the fabric onto it (Fig. 29a). (White PVA adhesive can be used as a heat bonding film; spread it on the mount, allow it to dry and then reactivate it with a domestic iron as you apply the fabric.) Turn the covered mount over and cut out the centre, leaving a 25 mm excess over the edges of the window. Mitre this surplus carefully into the corners, remembering that if you slit too far there is no remedy. Then remove the corners of the outer edges (Fig. 29b). Glue all eight flaps in place on the underside of the mount (as shown in Fig. 29c).

Instead of glueing the outer edges over you can simply trim them

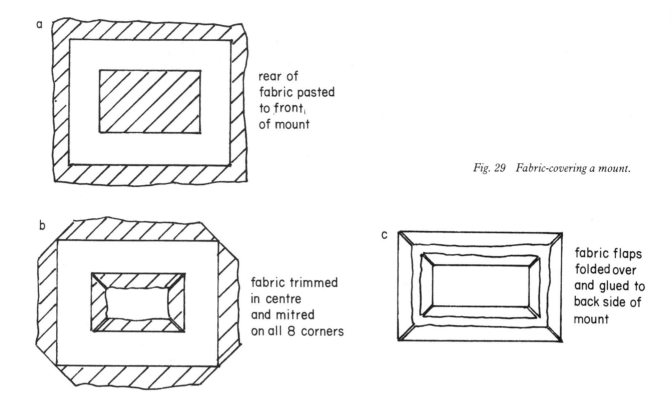

a   rear of
    fabric pasted
    to front
    of mount

Fig. 29   Fabric-covering a mount.

b   fabric trimmed
    in centre
    and mitred
    on all 8 corners

c   fabric flaps
    folded over
    and glued to
    back side of
    mount

flush with the edges of the mountboard, particularly if you are worried that your frame may not have the rebate depth to accommodate the excess folded over. It is not advisable, though, if your fabric frays easily or if the lip of your frame is narrow.

Silk, on account of its delicacy, is best not glued to the front of the board. You can simply glue the flaps, but this calls for more care in keeping the weave straight. Fabrics which will not take adhesive well can be sewn on the back (as shown in Fig. 30).

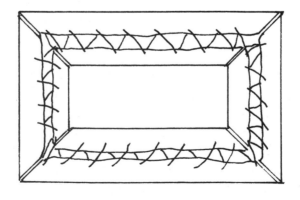

Fig. 30   Sewing a
fabric-covered mount.

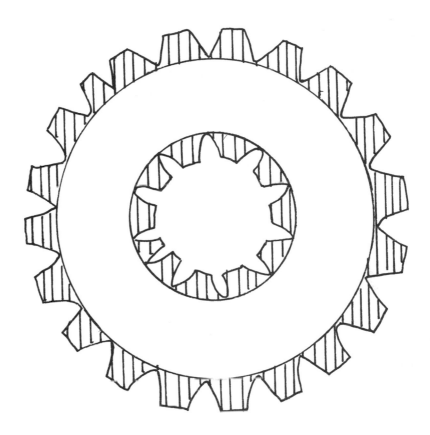

Fig. 31   *Tabbing a circular mount.*

Oval and circular mounts can be fabric-covered in the same way except that the inner and outer excess flaps must be tabbed rather than mitred (see Fig. 31).

FACING YOUR OWN MOUNTBOARD

If you do not like the range of colours offered by your local stockist it is easy to face your own mountboard. It can be done either by sticking a sheet of more interesting paper onto white mountboard or by painting it. (Any colour other than white will show that colour on the cut edge.)

Whether painting or laminating, remember to countermount, i.e to face the back side with a sheet of brown paper or similar to prevent the board bowing as it dries. Leave the board in a weighted, flattened position for all adhesive to dry out before trying to cut.

Painting mountboard is great fun. Water-based colours in gouache or acrylic are good to start with. Try applying them with a piece of (marine) sponge; this not only avoids the problem of visible

43

brushstrokes but leaves an interesting, faintly mottled texture. This technique can also be used to create subtle two-tone effects if you apply a light colour over a dark base; try light grey over dark blue, cream over brown, pink over charcoal.

If you become really hooked on this sort of experimentation you might progress to oil-based paints. Using a pale matte or eggshell paint as your base, you can tint small quantities of it with artists' oil colour and sponge it onto the board. Alternatively, dab evenly distributed strokes of two colours and blend them by sponging. For an even stronger mottled effect spatter the still-wet surface with fine droplets of white spirit.

NEEDLEWORK

Tapestry and embroidery will usually need to be stretched and squared onto a mount before framing. Wool tapestry is most likely to be out of true, particularly if it has been worked without a frame. Luckily it is fairly robust and can be coerced into position from the most unlikely angles. Embroidery, being more delicate, needs slightly more careful handling but is not often so deformed.

There are rack-like devices available from framing sundries suppliers which have toothed side members (held by corner plates) over which the needlework is progressively pulled and anchored (Fig. 32a). When fully stretched this toothed frame (into which you have put pre-cut hardboard) is put into the final frame. The disadvantage of this method, apart from cost, is that you must determine the stretched size of the piece before you start the operation, and you may find that you were wrong.

For the framer who only occasionally encounters this problem a piece of softboard and a box of pins will suffice. Using either a steam iron or a boiling kettle get the workpiece warm and damp and begin to stake it out on the softboard with long tacks or macramé pins (Fig. 32b). Use repeated applications of steam to stretch and re-stake it, testing the corners with a set square until you have it in shape. Leave it to cool and dry completely (several hours for a thick woollen tapestry) before removing the pins.

It can then be mounted onto hardboard. Any needlework with a thin or pale base fabric should go onto white-faced hardboard because darker colours will show through enough to dull the appearance. If you do not want the expense of buying laminated board paint it yourself or interleave a sheet of white card. (The appearance of some

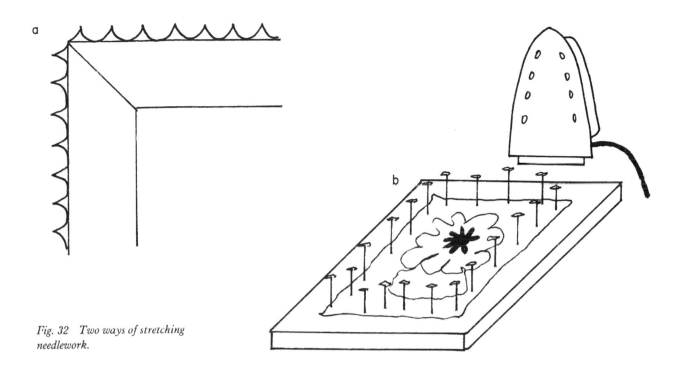

Fig. 32 *Two ways of stretching
needlework.*

framed needlework can be greatly enhanced by interleaving a sheet of
thin white foam to create a 'cushion effect'.)

You can glue the fabric to the board as with laid-down paper art but
this should not be done with anything valuable. It is usually sufficient
to fold the surplus fabric over the edge of the artboard and tape it taut
on the other side. If there is not sufficient border surplus sew
extension strips around the edge.

THREE-DIMENSIONAL ART

There is no less clumsy phrase which will suitably encompass the
range of small objects which may lend themselves to display within
frames (with or without glass). Coins, medals, jewellery, badges,
insignia, ceramics, keys, fishing flies and shells are but a few. Most
look best fixed to a background of plain fabric: velvet or silk for a rich,
cossetted effect, hessian or burlap for something a bit more robust.
Most benefit from a generous allocation of space between themselves
and the frame.

If you have an object which is decorated on both sides you might
consider the use of a mirror as backing to show it to fullest advantage.

For fabric-based mounting cut a piece of hardboard to the

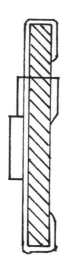

Fig. 33   Mounting a medal.

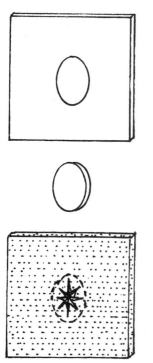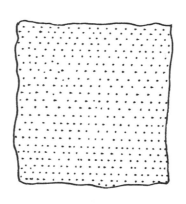

Fig. 34   Mounting a coin.

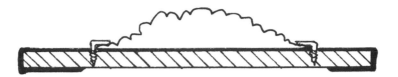

Fig. 35   Mounting three-dimensional objects with wire and screw turns.

appropriate size and mark on the back the point of fixture for the object. This is easier than trying to find the centre of a board that has already been covered in pale silk; simply poke a needle through from the back mark.

The fixing method depends on the nature of the object and whether or not you might one day want to remove it.

1) Medals with ribbons can be slung from the top edge of the mount or through slits cut part way down it (see Fig. 33).
2) Circular objects such as coins can be recessed into the backing. Mark and cut the aperture in the board before pasting on the fabric. Slit the fabric in a star shape (as shown in Fig. 34) and press the disc into place. This can work for other shapes if you can cut the aperture accurately enough.
3) Lightweight items can be sewn into place with 'invisible' thread. The suitability of this method depends on shape as well as weight.
4) Objects with a ferrous metal content can be held in place with self-adhesive magnetic strip.
5) Awkward objects which do not lend themselves to any other removable fixture may have to be glued. Double-sided foam tape is as strong as liquid adhesive and will take up minor irregularities in the back surface of the object, but if it is heavily contoured you may need a two-part adhesive. As always with adhesives, be guided by the manufacturer's advice on suitability for specific surfaces.
6) Valuable objects which one day may need to be cleanly removed cannot be glued. If thread will not hold try wire, pushed through the backboard and twisted. Sometimes screwturns (described in Chapter 8) are handy if the object is conveniently shaped (see Fig. 35).

4 · MOULDINGS

'Moulding' is the term used to describe the shaped wood (occasionally metal) used to make the frame. It derives from the days when the frame was usually covered with plasterwork moulding to simulate carved wood. Nowadays most suppliers offer a wide range of prefinished mouldings which have been factory-coated with coloured paint, plastic laminate or gilt substitute. Such finishes are often applied to wood of fairly poor quality but they will be nonetheless more expensive than mouldings in plain, unfinished timber of superior quality. Prefinished mouldings offer the home framer the tempting prospect of quick results but, in addition to their expense, they are most unforgiving of mistakes. A slightly gapped mitre, a rough edge or misplaced nail will be very hard to disguise against the factory finish.

Beginners are therefore strongly advised to start with raw timber mouldings. They are cheaper and can be obtained from a wider range of retail outlets. They offer ample opportunity for the remedy of constructional blunders; sanding, filling and the judicious application of stain and polish can hide a multitude of sins. These processes are easy to carry out – it is almost impossible to ruin a frame at the finishing stage – and the result will usually be more pleasing.

Before detailing the choice of wood and shape it should perhaps be noted that metal frames come in two categories (as shown in Fig 36). True metal frames are sometimes used in framing but they have constructional requirements beyond the scope of this book, because they must be mitred with a hacksaw and welded. 'Aluminium' (aluminum) frames are made from a wooden box-shaped moulding laminated with a skin of machined aluminium in silver, gold or bronze finish. Well-made frames of this type look extremely good on some modern prints and photography but their construction is not easy. The moulding is difficult to saw by hand and the slightest deformation of the metal skin makes for unsightly corners which cannot be easily remedied.

The timbers most commonly used for frame mouldings are straight-grained, knot-free hardwoods. Ramin is widely available in the UK. It is a pale straw-coloured wood from Sarawak and has a fairly undistinguished grain with very few knots. Its weight is medium and it cuts fairly easily though with a slight tendency to split. Jelutong, another tropical hardwood, looks similar but is lighter, knottier and

aluminium
skin on wood

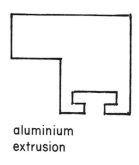

aluminium
extrusion

Fig. 36 Metal mouldings.

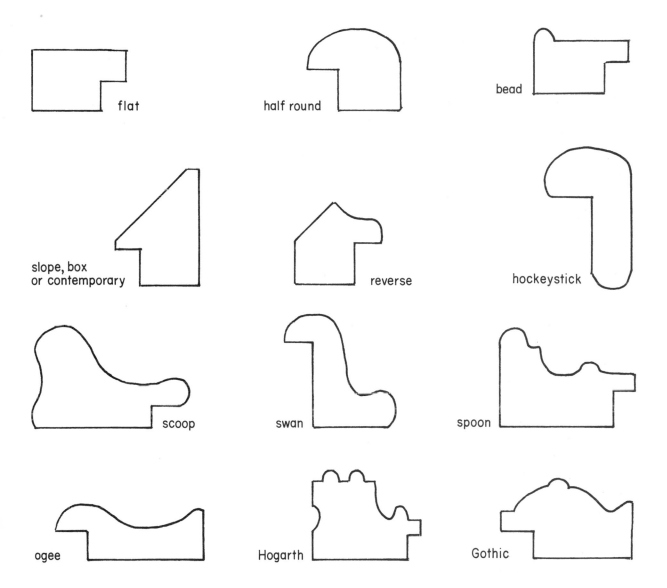

flat

half round

bead

slope, box
or contemporary

reverse

hockeystick

scoop

swan

spoon

ogee

Hogarth

Gothic

*Fig. 37 Common moulding profiles
in wood.*

spongier. Pine is sometimes used but its profusion of knots coupled
with its unsuitability for many finishes makes it of limited appeal.

In the USA basswood (from the lime or linden tree) is a common
choice for frames, often recommended to the beginner because it is
easy to work. Chestnut became popular some decades ago following a
massive worm attack on American chestnut trees rendering the wood
unfit for many structural purposes. 'Wormy chestnut' is still much
sought after in the States.

Oak still outclasses most other woods, having a handsome grain

49

which calls for no more than a good beeswax polish. In the past it has been fashionable to treat it with chloride of lime (unslaked) to give it a weathered, grey finish. It is however heavy, hard to saw by hand, expensive and difficult to obtain from retail outlets.

Mahogany can also be hard to find despite its suitability for framing. You may find mouldings in its 'bastard' relatives, such as virola or lauan, sold in homecraft and woodworking shops, sometimes masquerading as the more distinguised relative (although they are noticeably lighter). You are unlikely to find the finest Central American mahogany but African mahogany and the cheaper substitutes are fairly easy to work and polish beautifully.

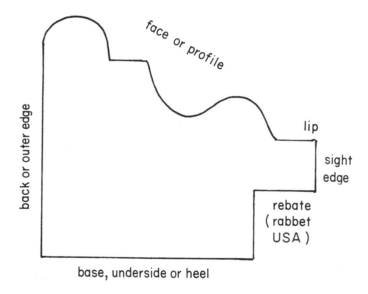

Fig. 38 *Moulding features.*

Of the two traditional English frame woods new walnut is now very hard to find in mouldings, and never in widths wider than 19 mm (¾ in). The other one, maple, is included in some prefinished ranges as a veneer; unfortunately it has often been coated with a cheap, sticky lacquer rather than the French polish which it deserves. Solid maple is obtainable from trade suppliers, either in the more expensive 'birdseye' version (from the sapwood of the rock maple) or in its slightly cheaper, regular grain form. Both are difficult to buy in unfinished timber.

Illustrated in Fig. 37 are the traditional shapes or profiles of picture frame mouldings, plus a diagram naming their features (Fig. 38). This terminology can be helpful if you are buying from a catalogue. There

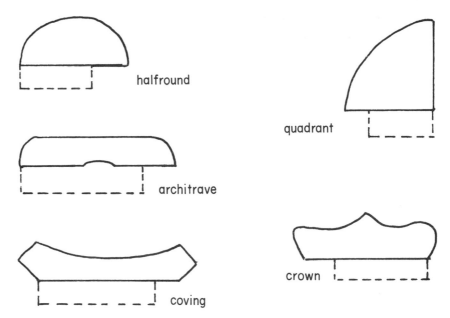

Fig. 39 Builders' mouldings which can be rebated for framing.

halfround

quadrant

architrave

coving

crown

can be some ambiguity in describing mouldings by size; a '19 mm spoon' will usually mean 19 mm (¾ in) across the widest part of the cross section, but in some catalogues the dimension will refer to height.

A specialist stockist will also offer slips or liners which are plain, shallow slope mouldings used as second, inner frames, often on an oil canvas where a mount would be inappropriate. Slips are often linen-covered and may have a gilded edge.

As well as using the purpose-designed picture frame mouldings you may care to experiment with builders' mouldings to produce frames with more unusual profiles (as shown in Fig. 39). These architectural mouldings usually lack a rebate (rabbet) so it will be necessary to buy a corresponding length of stripwood (say, 10 by 15 mm cross section) to glue to the underside of the moulding. If you cannot get the exact width you require you may end up with a wider lip than would normally be found on a picture frame moulding. This need not matter except that you may need to plan a larger frame in order to avoid losing too much of the edge of your picture under the moulding.

Carved beading, as used in the furniture trade, can also be converted to frame moulding by the addition of a rebate. This sort of stripwood is usually ramin in widths from 12 mm (½ in) to 50 mm (2 in) or wider in a variety of machine-carved patterns, examples of which are illustrated in Fig. 40. Although many are too ornate for use on

51

pictures they can make decorative mirror frames. This beading is
available from many homecraft shops or from the trade suppliers listed
in the Appendix.

*Fig. 40 Carved beading which can
be rebated for framing.*

WHAT TYPE TO BUY

In choosing a moulding for a particular picture there are several points
to bear in mind. Firstly of course there is the aesthetic question of a
profile which complements the picture. The more traditional shapes
tend to have curves and softer contours. Obviously these would be at
variance with a modern image of starkly angled lines which would be
happier in, say, a simple box or slope moulding. Hogarth, a narrow,
spoon-shaped moulding in black and gold (sometimes brown and
cream) is a modern copy of an eighteenth-century style and is widely
used on old prints – so much so in fact that it now tends to look
something of a stereotype.

   You will of course need to try a sample (preferably a mitred corner)
of the moulding against your picture, with the mount if one is to be
used. View it both close to and from a distance. Placing the moulding
on a number of different pictures as well as the one which you intend
to frame may help you to discern its less obvious characteristics.

   You must also take into account the physical requirements of the
frame. Some authorities specify that the width of the moulding should
not be less than one twentieth of the longest side of the mounted
picture or the finished frame will not be able to take the weight. The
bottom of the frame may bend downwards or at worst one of the
mitres may collapse. This dictum is quite widely disregarded but you

would do well to bear it in mind. There are ways of strengthening a weak frame, described in Chapter 9, but they are better employed as remedies on old frames rather than constructional techniques.

Secondly you must check that the rebate of the chosen moulding is sufficient to take the 'sandwich' of art, mount and backing. Depths vary but 8 mm is fairly frequently found on medium-sized mouldings and 5 mm on the narrow ones. 5 mm will not take 2 mm glass, 6-sheet mountboard, cartridge paper, card backing and hardboard and still leave enough depth for standard back fixings such as brads. The problem of contents which protrude out of the back of the frame is not insoluble (see Chapter 8) but it is as well to be aware of the situation at the decision stage.

Lastly you must consider the limitations of your equipment. Obviously you must not choose a moulding which is too deep for your mitre box or saw. It would also be a good idea to avoid 'shellback' mouldings, i.e. those which do not have a substantial vertical back. This perpendicular surface is vital for firm clamping when you saw and nail the frame. Examples of shellbacks in Fig. 37 are the swan and the scoop.

Fig. 41 Calculating the required length of moulding.

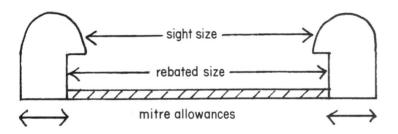

HOW MUCH TO BUY

It is tempting to aim for exactitude in buying wood for a frame but this is not a good idea. It is far better to err on the generous side than to find yourself a few inches short because you had to recut a poor mitre. Leftover lengths can be used for photo frames or, if they are in raw timber, for experiments in staining and finishing.

In calculating the lengths required you begin with the rebated size of your picture, that is to say the sight or view size plus the tiny border beyond it which will be concealed by the lip of the frame (see Fig. 41). To this must be added:

1) a small allowance for fit − 3 mm per length should be ample;
2) the mitre allowance, which is twice the base width of the moulding;
3) at least 50 mm (2 in) per length for comfortable cutting room. This is a bare minimum; better still to add a bit more to allow for false starts, defective arithmetic etc.

WHERE TO BUY

Your source of supply may be somewhat limited. Most commercial framers will sell footage from their stock but they will charge top price because they are not in the business of encouraging home framing. For the unambitious home framer they will offer a mitring service but this will not do much for your sense of achievement. It might be worth considering, however, if you are using a shellback.

The large homecraft superstores in the UK now carry a range of prefinished mouldings and (usually sold separately) a selection of raw timber mouldings with and without rebates. These latter will commonly be in ramin with a few in virola or lauan. Prices will be more competitive but you will have to buy a standard length of around 2.5 m (about 8 ft) and of course there will be no mitring service or professional advice on offer.

Small woodworking shops are fast disappearing under this competition but remain an excellent source of choice and service. They may not mitre but will often sell small footage or at least chop standard lengths into easily manageable pieces. They also tend to have bins of odd lengths going cheap from which small pictures can be framed very cheaply indeed.

Timber merchants or lumber-yards usually carry some raw wood mouldings for framing and, of course, a good selection of architectural mouldings.

In the USA there is a growing spread of craft centres where amateur framers can not only buy their materials but rent access to equipment and expertise as well. There are also extensive mail order facilities in the States; they can be traced through craft and hobby magazines.

Trade suppliers are well worth researching when you reach the stage of framing regularly. Most will not be fussy about your lack of commercial status provided that you meet their minimum order requirements, which may be in quantity or order value. They are, of course, dramatically cheaper than retail outlets; savings can often be in the order of 60 or 70 per cent. Prices quoted will of course be subject to carriage and possibly taxes. If you submit an enquiry and ask for a proforma invoice (advance payment is normally required from small customers) you will see the full total and be able to calculate the gross cost per foot. Most trade suppliers specify a 50 foot minimum order quantity, but if you are able to go to a trade counter and collect you may be able to negotiate down from this.

The disadvantage of buying at a distance is that you cannot handpick your lengths. Raw wood mouldings in particular are likely to have defects and a small number in a bulk consignment is to be expected. If, however, you feel that they are so numerous as to render a substantial quantity of the wood unusable you will have to negotiate the return of the goods and their replacement.

If you are choosing your own lengths watch out for the following.

1) Warped lengths: these are particularly likely where wood is stored on its end rather than in horizontal racking.

2) Splits: damaged ends are common but make sure, particularly with ramin, that the splits do not run along the edge of a thin contour feature such as the lip or a ridge.

3) Cutter marks: these are caused by careless routeing when the cutter judders and creates a series of ridges across the width of the face. They may not be very noticeable when the wood is in its raw state — more easily felt by finger than seen — but they will become more prominent under stain and polish. Unlike natural blemishes which can impart a pleasing antique look, their crosswise regularity makes them unsightly and difficult to disguise. Paint does not wholly conceal them either.

4) Sap streaks: these are natural streaks of darker colour which may take stain unevenly.

5) Knots: these will have to be treated with knotting compound before the wood is painted or polished (but not before staining because stain will not 'take' through the seal created by the knotting) to prevent leakage of resin through to the finish. Dead knots (the black ones) may even fall out and leave a hole. The problem is unlikely to arise with any timber other than pine. If you do buy knotty wood, intending to use the knots as a feature, choose pieces in which the knots are fairly evenly distributed; a

concentration of knots in one or two members of the frame while the other two are clear will look unbalanced.

6) Woodworm: watch out for odd holes. You are not likely to find a major infestation in new timber but it is not a good idea to bring any doubtful timber in contact with other mouldings you may have.

When choosing more than one length of raw timber for a single frame match your lengths to ensure, as far as possible, that they all came from the same batch. Careless stocking of the racks can mix lengths of the same wood differing quite markedly in colour if they were cut from different consignments. Such differences can be more pronounced with stain and polish.

Profiles can differ marginally too. The manufacturer's cutters are constantly being reset for successive batches and may not always be reset consistently for the same profile. Such differences may not be noticeable to a casual glance but will show up clearly on a mitred corner.

As your standards and expectations rise you may become impatient with the quality and limited range of mouldings on general commercial offer. Producing your own calls for skills beyond the scope of this book. You may, however, be lucky enough to find a local woodworker or furniture maker who will produce mouldings to your design specification. The cost will be at least as expensive as retail prices and the minimum order quantity on a par with trade suppliers so it might not seem like a good deal but you will have the satisfaction of having created a unique moulding design and the opportunity of having it produced in an unusual wood such as cherry or yew.

5 · BASIC FRAME CONSTRUCTION

Now that you have chosen and purchased your materials you now approach that bugbear of all amateur framers – the execution of the perfect 45 degree sawcut. If you can meet this challenge it is safe to say that no subsequent operation in the picture framing process is likely to cause you much trouble. If you get it wrong, you can fudge to some extent but your frame will always be fundamentally unsound.

MITRE CUTTING

There are several pieces of equipment available to help you. It goes without saying that in buying your tools you should choose the best that you can afford from a well known manufacturer. Your saw should be a tenon or fine back saw with at least 16 (and preferably 24) points to the inch. Use it for nothing else but sawing mouldings. These saws come in several sizes governing the depth of moulding that they can cut. Make sure you buy one large enough for your needs.

The most basic mitring jig is the mitre box as shown in Fig. 42.

Fig. 42 Hand saw and wooden mitre box.

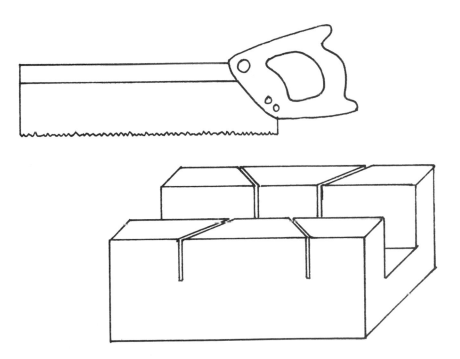

Usually it is made of beechwood but plastic ones are now appearing on the market. Wooden ones, though sturdier, are liable to erosion in the mitre slots and with time these will enlarge and give a less than accurate holding for the saw.

The moulding is clamped into the bed of the box with its base to bottom and lip facing into the centre of the box. The saw is used through the angled slits. The depth of these slits defines the depth of moulding that can be used in the box so these should also be taken into consideration when choosing your size of saw.

A metal mitre block (illustrated in Fig. 43) is a better long term investment. It does not wear and will also double as a corner cramp if at some time you want to fix individual mitres. Only one mitre can be cut at a time but the adjustable saw guides allow the use of deeper mouldings and saws. As with most of the cheaper equipment the maximum width of moulding that it will take is about 75 mm (3 in).

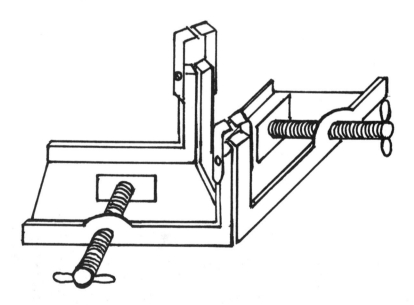

Fig. 43   Metal mitre block.

The next stage in sawing sophistication is the hand mitre saw (Fig. 44). A hand saw is fixed into a sawing bed such that it can swivel and be locked into a chosen angle on either side. Most of these can take mouldings up to 85 or 90 mm (around 3¾ in).

Professional framers use either a large, variable-angle, circular-bladed saw or a guillotine which notch-cuts two mitre faces at once. These can be electrically or pneumatically powered and are well beyond the budget of the amateur framer.

Whether you are using a box or metal block it should be securely

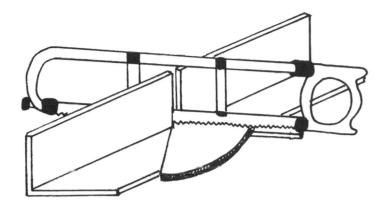

Fig. 44   Hand mitre saw.

clamped to the bench at a comfortable sawing height. If you have an adjustable-jaw workbench you can mount the jig onto a wooden block and clamp it between the jaws.

It may be convenient (thought slightly more wasteful) to pre-cut your moulding into handy lengths, each a few centimetres longer than you will need. This is better than having an extended piece of moulding hanging unsupported as you saw.

Pencil marks for sawing should be made on the top edge of the moulding (use well sharpened chalk on a prefinished moulding). This means that to the required rebated length you must add twice the

Mitre block clamped in the jaws of a purpose-built workbench.

width of the moulding base as described in Chapter 4. It goes without saying that you must aim for 100 per cent accuracy. If you are cutting several lengths of the same size it may be more convenient to bolt a stop in position and use this as your length guide.

If you are using a wooden mitre box you will need G-clamps (C-clamps) to hold the moulding in position. Some types of cutter have their own inbuilt clamps. Apply the clamp against the rebate (not the lip) and use a block of scrap wood in between to avoid marking the moulding. For the inbuilt clamp you will need scrap protecting both sides of the moulding if the wall behind the clamp is slightly recessed because a lightweight moulding may be deformed into it.

It is also a good idea to rest the base of the moulding on another piece of scrap stripwood so that there is no splitting of the underside as the saw breaks through. In a metal block it also helps prevent the saw blade being dulled against the metal (although in theory the saw guides, if correctly set, should stop this).

Stand squarely to the workpiece and draw the saw backwards two or three times to start the cut (known as the kerf). Then, holding the saw in your right hand, with the index finger extended along it, use the forward strokes only to deepen the cut. Try not to bear down too hard

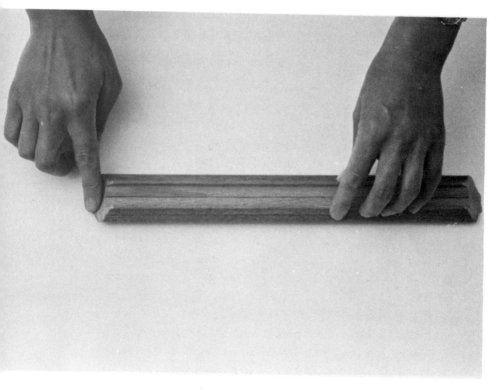

Checking pairs for identical length.

Checking the internal angles of the frame before glueing.

or you will tend to influence the vertical angle (90 degrees) of the cut to one side or another. The weight of the saw and the regularity of the stroke should be sufficient. It will seem like hard work if you are unused to the action, particularly if the moulding is thick.

The saw guides will help to keep you straight, but even within them there is scope for inaccuracy if you allow your hand pressure to tilt from one side to another. Remember that you are striving for accuracy in two planes: in the horizontal plane you are keeping your saw cut at 45 degrees to the line of the wood and in the vertical plane you are aiming to keep the cut exactly perpendicular.

Having sawn your four members lie the two pairs back down on a smooth flat surface as illustrated to check for length. This is better done by feel than by sight. Run your fingertip over the pair of upturned faces and adjust them until they feel as one surface. Without moving the pieces check that the other end feels the same. No matter how perfectly you have cut your 45 degree angle the mitres will gap if one side is a couple of millimetres longer than its partner.

Test your angular accuracy by clamping the (dry) corners and placing a setsquare on either the rebated interior or the exterior of the corner (accessibility will depend on your clamping device). One wrong angle will offset all the others because, no matter the length of its sides, the angles within a four-sided figure must add up to 360 degrees. If one is less than 90 degrees another must gap.

61

CONSTRUCTIONAL FAULTS

It is essential to identify these in the 'dry run' clamping exercise; once you have applied adhesive to the ends of the moulding you have very little time in which to determine the cause of any problem, let alone devise a remedy.

The faults that you are likely to come across are illustrated in Fig. 45 a to f.

Mitre gapping on the face (a and b): could be due to either:
  i) inaccurately sawn angles: check that the saw cut was a true vertical (usually fairly obvious on close inspection) and that, on the horizontal plane, it was exactly 45 degrees. Use a protractor or a setsquare.
  ii) non-identical pairs: you will probably find one member fractionally longer or shorter than its partner.

The only answer in either case is either to re-saw the offending piece or to cut new wood if this would mean an unacceptable reduction in the size of the frame.

Horizontally offset corner (c): this should be fairly easy to manipulate back into place unless it has been caused by a warped piece of moulding.

Mitre gapping at the back or base (d): the causes are as described in i) and ii) above but as it is less noticeable you may decide, if only a very small gap is involved, to press on regardless. Pack the gap with as much adhesive as you can get in and follow up with a filler after nailing. If you are using a belt cramp as shown in the illustration you might be able to effect some improvement by sliding the existing cramp higher and applying another set lower down.

Vertically offset corner (e): this can happen as you tighten the cramp, particularly if there is a lot of adhesive in that corner aiding the slippage. It does not imply any inaccuracy in sawing (although it may indicate a warped piece of moulding). More often than not you can manipulate it down but watch out for a recurrence of the problem while the adhesive is drying. It does not seriously compromise the strength of the frame but it looks careless and the corresponding step inside the rebated corner can make it difficult to get the glass to lie flat.

Frame will not lie flat (f): all frames should be tested for flatness by placing them, when clamped, on a true surface such as a mirror or piece of thick glass. If the frame rocks it may be that you have an inaccurately sawn length but that the force of your clamping method has nonetheless succeeded in closing the mitres. If this is

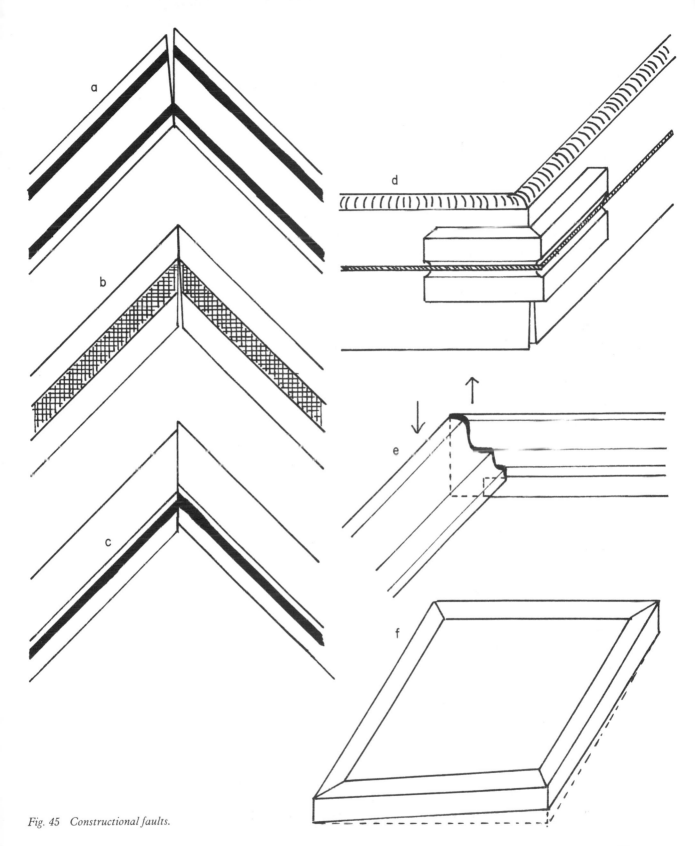

Fig. 45   Constructional faults.

63

not the problem then your wood must be warped. You may be able to persuade it back to the horizontal with a brick on each corner for a day or two.

SANDING AND STAINING

When you have established that your cut pieces will form a perfect rectangle you can heave a sigh of relief and proceed. If you are working in raw wood do the sanding now. You may need to sand the corners lightly again later but the bulk of the work should be done now, rather than rough-handling the assembled frame. Always sand with the grain and never across the moulding. Be careful not to sand the mitre faces or you will alter the angle.

If you are intending to stain the wood now is the best time. If you leave it until the frame is complete you will almost certainly have smeared some adhesive near the corners and this will prevent the wood from taking the stain, leaving tell-tale pale patches. Careful sanding can clear away a lot of this excess adhesive but when it has penetrated the grain within the contours of a corner it is almost impossible to remove in its entirety.

Homecraft shops offer two basic types of liquid stain. One can be diluted with water and one with white spirit. They have comparable colour ranges and both are equally suitable for frame wood. Some people find that the water-based colours are deeper and more natural; on the other hand water tends to raise the grain, calling for a second sanding operation. The two types are not compatible; if you have coloured your wood with, say, the water-diluted type and wish to modify the shade you cannot then do so with the white spirit type. Within each range, however, you can mix shades to create colours of your own preference. Four basic colours — a cold brown, a rosewood, a reddish brown and a yellow — should be enough to mix almost any shade of brown that you could want. Do note the proportions you have used though; it is most frustrating to run out of stain halfway round a large frame and find yourself unable to remember what went in to make the colour. With spirit stain, in particular, the wet edge does not stay 'live' for long, and delays in completion will mean tidemarks.

Stain can be applied with a brush or cloth. It is best to wear rubber gloves.

There is of course no real need to stain anything other than the face, lip and back of the moulding unless you are framing a mirror, in which case you must also colour under the lip and down the inside edge of

64

the rebate. If this is left the raw wood will reflect from the edges of the mirror and be visible.

Think twice, however, before applying stain to a really fine wood. A commonplace timber such as ramin takes it well and is versatile in that you can make it impersonate all sorts of superior woods (albeit without the grain) by judicious use of stain and polish. Oak and mahogany, on the other hand, have a fine colour of their own which can be gently deepened with linseed oil and wax polish at the finishing stage. Some forms of oak positively resist chemical stain and look quite nasty if you try to force it on them.

Allow the stain to dry fully before corner fixing. If corner cramps are applied while the wood is still damp it will dry a slightly different colour in those areas covered by the cramps.

GLUEING AND CLAMPING

The mitred corners of the frame need both glue and nails to keep them securely fixed. Some clamping devices claim to hold the corners such that nails or pins can be driven in before the glue has dried. This is certainly true of professional clamping equipment for with the advent of while-you-wait framing services it became a commercial necessity. The novice, however, would be advised to regard glueing and

Fig. 46 One corner cramp.

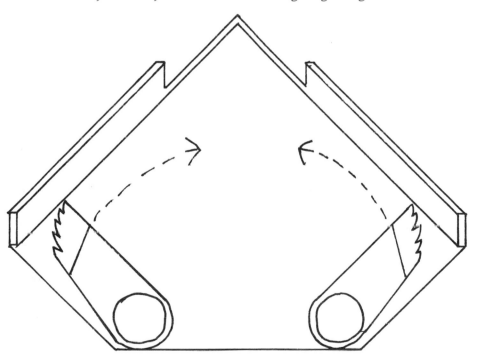

65

clamping as two separate operations.

Traditional cabinetmaker's or 'Scotch' glue came in the form of pearl granules which had to be stewed up on a workshop gas ring. This has now been superseded by modern PVA adhesives; any good brand designated as woodworking glue will suffice. Apply it as directed on the container but not before you have tested your clamping method in a dry run to be sure that you can bring the surfaces together without delay when the adhesive has been applied.

Various methods of clamping are available through homecraft shops. The following three types illustrate the basic principles by which it can be done.

1) Corner clamps: four plastic corner pieces each with two spring-loaded levers which hold the rebated corner. These clamps will not take the larger mouldings and are not easy to use accurately. A single clamp is shown in Fig 46.
2) Belt clamp: this consists of four moulded plastic corners with grooved outer edges to take a nylon cord running around the frame. It is pulled tight and anchored in a toggle (Fig. 47a). This is by far the easiest and cheapest method; you can even make your own version. Some more sophisticated versions based on the same principle have a handle in the corner for tautening the cord.
3) 'Jaws' clamp: four metal jaws are applied to the corners and are joined in the centre with a wing nut which pulls them together (Fig. 47b).

Fig. 47 Belt clamp and 'jaws' clamp.

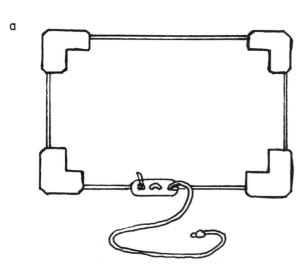

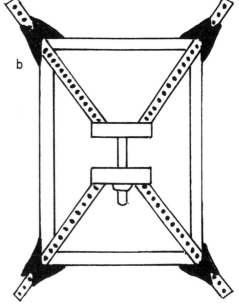

In extremis you can of course try using adhesive tape (non-stretch) as shown in Fig. 48, but this does not really apply the pressure that is needed to make firm joints.

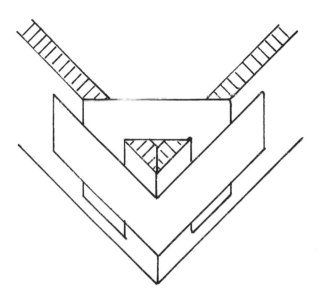

Fig. 48 Desperate measures: adhesive tape instead of a clamp.

In the next league you find mitre vices which tilt to present each corner in the best position for nailing (which in this case is done straight after the application of adhesive). Examples of this type are considerably more expensive than the equipment described previously. For mass production there are powered 'underpinners' which press the corners together and fire metal jointing plates in from underneath.

One method frequently recommended to beginners is to fix one member vertically in a bench vice, dab adhesive on the end, present the next member, slightly offset above the required position and, holding this with one hand, use the other to hammer in a nail. The effect of the hammer blows will, of course, dislodge the second member from its position but the theory is that the original offset will have accounted for this and the mitre will come miraculously into place. Whoever devised this method did not have the best interests of amateurs at heart; it is a recipe for disaster, bad temper and smashed mitres.

Unless you have a tilting mitre vice it is far better to glue all four corners, clamp, and wait for the adhesive to dry before nailing. (Be sure, incidentally, that you are not joining two members of the same

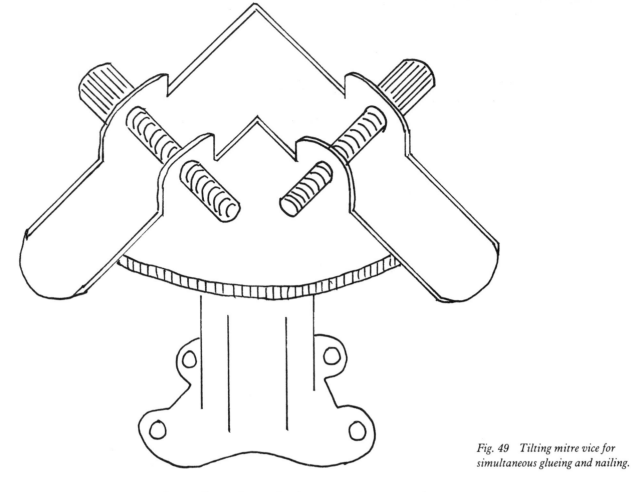

Fig. 49   Tilting mitre vice for simultaneous glueing and nailing.

length – easy to do if your frame is nearly, but not quite, square.)
When you have fastened your clamping device wipe off any excess
adhesive which has squeezed out of the joints. Pay particular attention
to the contoured face (a cotton wool bud dampened in white spirit is
handy) because this will be difficult to scrape clean once the adhesive
has dried.

You must allow the full drying time recommended by the adhesive
manufacturer. If the adhesive still looks white rather than transparent
it is too soon. When the time comes to remove the clamps your frame
will be firm but it will not survive rough handling or accidental drops,
so keep it well supported.

NAILING

The best nails to use are panel pins, in length about 75 per cent of the
moulding width. Oval panel pins minimise the risk of splitting near
the edges of the wood. One pin per corner will be enough for a small

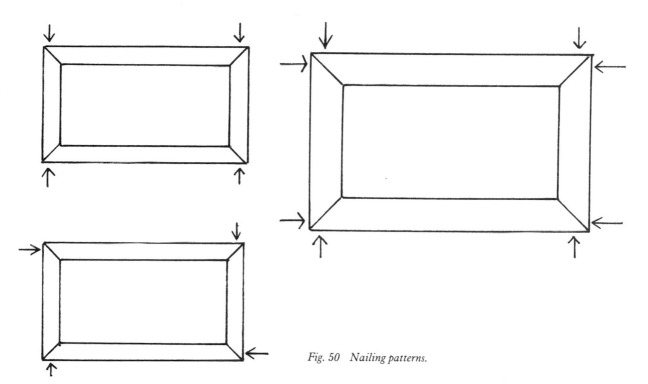

Fig. 50   Nailing patterns.

lightweight frame (there may not be room for more) but most frames will need two. Some schools of thought prescribe nailing down from the top and up from the bottom on the grounds that this leaves the visible sides unblemished. Others prefer to nail from all angles as shown in Fig. 50. If you adopt this latter method make sure that your second nail will not collide with the first as you drive it in.

Clamping the frame for hammering can be done in a variety of ways but it is important that your method gives support to the second member into which the nail is driven rather than the first. Otherwise the nail may simply push the two apart. You can use an inbuilt-clamp type of mitre block or simply clamp the frame to the workbench in a vice. Protect the frame from the jaws with scrap wood and avoid using the clamp on the face of the moulding (but if you must, protect it with a piece of thick stout fabric such as carpet underfelt). Remember that the lip cannot take any pressure.

If a large frame is being held horizontally by one corner it must be given some other support and not left hanging while being hammered.

Frames in very sturdy mouldings can even be nailed without clamping if you are very sure of your adhesive bond. Simply stand them on the floor or workbench and drive in nails from the top, steadying with your hand.

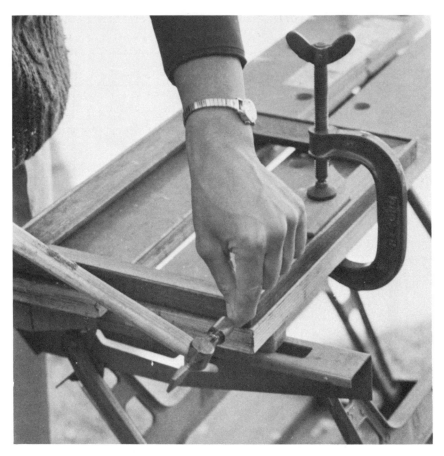

The nailing process can be a fairly hazardous one from the point of view of the health of the frame. It is worth spending some time and effort on devising a sound method of holding the frame because the consequences of failure can be most discouraging. A misdriven nail can be remedied (see next paragraph), but if your hammer blows cause the adhesive bond to fracture you have no alternative but to open up all four mitres, clean them down (because the glue will not work on dried residues) and start again. You cannot refix one corner in isolation because the movement weakens the others; nor can you drive home the nails in the hopes that they will hold the mitre soundly without benefit of adhesive. There will always be a minuscule amount of movement.

Start a hole for your nails with a sharp tool such as a gimlet or birdcage awl. When hammering, use a small tack hammer and make sure you are aiming straight. If the nail starts to bend, pull it out with pincers and start with a fresh one rather than trying to correct it.

Beware at all times of the nail tip coming out on the surface of the moulding. If this does happen you may be able to depress it with the hammer and nailset but it is better to extract it if possible. Apply the nailset to the tip of the nail in line with it and hammer it gently out backwards. The damaged surface can be sanded gently and filled. Your problem is that if you start with another nail in the same hole it will tend to follow the path of the old one, so re-site the second nail if possible (or use a shorter one).

As each nail is hammered home its head should be sunk below the surface of the wood with the nailset, creating a small hole which will later be hidden. When the frame is finished you should be able to run your fingers over these holes and feel nothing.

Your frame is now as strong as it will ever be but you should still not take liberties with it. Do not hang it from a corner and do not drop it.

FINISHING

The finishing and titivating operation now begins in earnest. Using a sharp blade, clear the corners of any dried adhesive. The rebated inside needs as much attention as the outside, because blobs here will prevent the glass from lying flat. It is possible to remedy minor geometric inaccuracies with this sort of bladework; a slightly overlapped corner, for example, can be judiciously pared. Beware of over-enthusiasm for this, though, or you will end up with a frame that looks as though it had hand-carved corners.

The nail holes and any small gaps can now be filled with wood filler. Several brands are available, most of which boldly claim to 'take stain'. They do, to some extent, but not in the same way that wood does. If you have not yet stained your wood you should be careful not to wipe any filler into the grain around the filled areas or you will have obvious paler patches. Most fillers come in a range of colours which label themselves as 'cedar', 'light oak', 'mahogany' etc, but they are not close natural matches. Since filler does not keep particularly well you would probably be better off keeping one pale natural shade and touching up with acrylic paint.

When the filler has dried you can do your final sanding operation, using medium grade paper on the corners and finishing with flour paper all over until the whole of the moulding is silky smooth.

(These cosmetic operations, of course, are not open to the user of prefinished mouldings. The most that can be done to these is to fill and touch up the nail holes.)

If your sanding has lightened the stain too much (perhaps on the corners) you can apply a second coat. If you want to lighten the colour instead you can sand, or rub down with white spirit (assuming you have used a spirit stain). In fact the more you experiment with rubbing down and refinishing the more you will achieve a mature, if not actually antique, look to your frame.

If you are intending to French polish you may decide to use a grain filler. It will also impart a softer feel to any coarse-grained wood that you simply want to wax. Proprietary brands are on sale but are not always easy to find. You can make your own by mixing gesso (from an art shop) with linseed oil. Rub the filler well in, across and with the grain, with a soft cloth. Then take a fresh piece of cloth and rub hard to remove all surface excess. Make sure you do not have a build-up along any ridges or channels in the face of the moulding.

The filler will take 2 – 24 hours to dry depending on its composition, after which it should be rubbed down with fine grade steel wool. This can be bought from homecraft stores and is graded 000 (the finest), 00, 0, 1, 2 etc upwards.

You can now finish either with linseed oil and beeswax to give a soft natural sheen or you can get a higher gloss with French polish. French polish, button polish and white polish are similar preparations based on shellac and methylated spirit. The proverbial grand piano finish is beyond the reach of most amateurs; nonetheless a modest shine can be worked up by anyone. Use a lint-free cotton cloth twisted around some cotton wool (not medicated) to form the 'rubber' and apply the polish with this using firm strokes along the grain. Being methylated spirit based the polish dries very fast and in the early stages is absorbed by the wood. You can work slowly round the frame fairly continuously for about three laps; then you will feel a sticky 'pull'.

It is now time to stop and let the polish dry for a while. (This should be done in a dry, warmish, dust-free atmosphere.) After about thirty minutes, go over the frame with 000 grade steel wool and dust it off thoroughly. Then apply a couple more coats of polish with the rubber. You can continue this process for as long as you like – the finish will get better and better provided that you can bring yourself to use the steel wool courageously. It feels like taking one step forward and two steps back, but it is an essential part of the process. If you find the polish is building up unevenly, or that a dribble has dried, tackle the problem with a cotton wool bud dipped in methylated spirit.

The final coat is applied with a 50:50 mixture of methylated spirit and polish (some would say with spirit alone) on the rubber, which is used in one bold stroke across each surface of the moulding, leaving a really high gloss finish. Leave the frame for some hours afterwards to dry thoroughly, before polishing with good furniture wax (not silicone). If the gloss is a little too high for your liking apply the wax with steel wool.

French polishing is surrounded by a great deal of mystique and many would say that the process described above is too oversimplified to be true French polish at all. Nonetheless it works and it does not take a lifetime's apprenticeship to master. The wood is protected and the feel is infinitely superior to polyurethane varnish. (Such varnish, in any case, is not well suited to ramin and some other tropical hardwoods whose surface characteristics inhibit the drying process.)

French polish, being based on orange shellac, will modify the final colour of your frame towards a warm brown. Button polish is based on yellow shellac. White polish (harder to find) is milky-transparent and is used for light-coloured woods. Ebonising is a high gloss black polish achieved with lampblack powder mixed into French polish. You can get a similar, if coarser, effect with black powder paint. Strain it through a piece of fine cotton before use if it looks gritty. Wood to be ebonised should be stained black first.

If you decide to paint your frame instead you can use almost any kind of paint intended for wood but there are several considerations which favour acrylic paint.

1) It is self priming.
2) It is water-based which simplifies brush cleaning and lessens the drying time between coats.
3) It is easy and economical to mix colours if you want to achieve a specific shade.
4) It dries matte which may be more pleasing than the gloss of enamel paint, but if you wish you can apply another coat of matte, mid-sheen or gloss varnish.

On the debit side it does not come off with paint stripper should you later change your mind. Ordinary decorator's gloss paint does little to enhance frames; white gloss in particular does not age gracefully. Eggshell paint looks attractive but is difficult to find in a good choice of colours. You can in fact brew up your own colours using artist's oil colour as a stainer and mixing it with oil-based paint. Water-based emulsions can be coloured with poster paint. You might also try other techniques such as:

1) painting a flat background colour (matte black, say) and, when dry, overcoating with another colour (light grey, perhaps) and then rubbing it off while still wet with a cloth so that it remains only in the grain;
2) 'combing' the paint after application to give it a lined pattern;
3) applying paint with a (marine) sponge to give a different texture;
4) spattering a second colour on top of a background coat: dip a toothbrush in the spatter colour and draw a small stick across the bristles to flick droplets all over the frame.

These methods are best tried out on scrap wood first, not only to assess the resulting appearance but to determine the optimum thickness of paint to use. If you use water-based emulsion you can quickly wash off anything you do not like. The final effect can later be varnished (painted ramin does not, of course, disagree with polyurethane varnish).

Gold always has been and still is a favourite finish for frames. The traditional gilding process involves a great deal of time, skill and expense and is outside the scope of this book. Suffice to say that it involves successive coats of gesso, red clay, shellac and gold size before the final application of the delicate, hideously expensive leaves. Each of these is about one three-hundred-thousandth of an inch thick and needs careful, practised handling. Finally the surface is burnished. The natural authentic sheen of gold leaf lasts for hundreds of years in sympathetic conditions and knocks into a cocked hat all modern attempts to create a substitute.

Therefore it is perhaps better not to aim for a brilliant gold finish on large areas. The result will almost certainly look garish and brassy. Various gold (and silver) paints are available through craft shops and art stores; they differ widely in their appearance and you must experiment to find your own preference. A superior effect can be obtained with a gold-pigmented wax product (soluble in white spirit). Trial and error is again the only method because it does not 'take' readily on all surfaces.

One way of using gold paint discreetly is to apply it very thinly over a coloured base coat of stain or paint, rubbing down to let the base colour show through. The wax product can look good applied over either a warm brown stain or a base coat of red or green acrylic paint. It is best put on by finger very carefully in small quantities − dabbing, almost rather than smearing. You can spread it with a spirit-dampened cloth but it then tends to look more like paint.

Most of the foregoing applies also to silver, except of course that it is more suited to base colours such as black, grey and blue, rather than brown, red and green.

Having achieved a finish that satisfies you do give it plenty of time to dry. It is very tempting to slip the frame over the picture to get a preview of the final effect but you run the risk of marking the edge of your mount or picture, so be patient. Mirror frames should have the finish taken under the lip and a little way down into the rebate because this area will be reflected into view by the glass. The base or underside need not be finished because it will be covered by the tape seal, unless the frame is intended to have removable back fixtures.

6 · VARIATIONS ON THE BASIC THEME

Once you have acquired the skill and equipment to make standard frames you can consider branching out into some novelty forms. This is the sort of work which the professional high-speed franchise framer is reluctant to undertake.

Most of these types of frame were briefly outlined and illustrated in Chapter 1. This section gives more constructional detail.

BAGUETTE

This is even simpler than a standard frame because it has no mitres! Baguettes are used on modern, unglazed art where the requirement is for nothing more than edge protection. They have the advantage of being slightly more forgiving of an out-of-square stretcher or panel.

Choose a width of plain stripwood that is about 6 mm (¼ in) wider

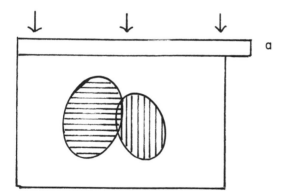

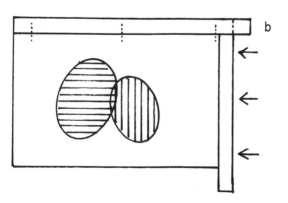

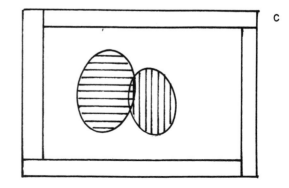

Fig. 51   Making a baguette.

than the depth of the stretcher. This extra 6 mm will project forwards from the face of the art and protect it from any frontal impact if it is dropped face down or anything is leaned against it.

Saw a length a few centimetres longer than one side of the stretcher. Fix it to the stretcher, as illustrated in Fig. 51, with the left-hand end flush and the surplus extending to the right. Nails are often recommended for this fixture but they can make the baguette difficult to remove at a later date. Screws are better, if a little more trouble. Use flat-headed ones which can be countersunk out of sight and filled over.

Then apply the second length in the same way (Fig. 51b). When this second side is in place you can saw off the projection of the first side flush with the edge to make a lapped or butt joint. Continue in the same fashion all the way round.

Baguettes are frequently left in the natural wood colour. If you want to paint or polish it, it is better to do so before you start fixing to the stretcher, but you will of course have to touch up your sawn edges and countersunk screw holes.

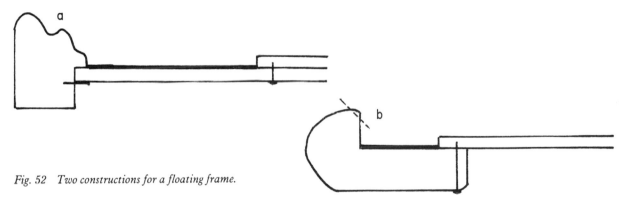

Fig. 52   Two constructions for a floating frame.

FLOATING FRAME

A floating frame incorporates a flat strip (usually black) between the frame and a canvas or block-mounted picture. The visual effect is to free the art from the constricting appearance of the frame and allow it to 'float' out towards the viewer. This can be done by screwing or nailing both the outer frame and the stretcher (with or without inner frame depending upon the condition of its edges) to a background of painted plywood or hardboard (as shown in Fig. 52a).

An alternative, quicker method if you only want a very narrow field of black is to use a deep-rebated moulding turned on to its back, as shown in Fig. 52b, and to paint the upended rebate black. You might have to sand or plane the upturned sight edge if it looks too sharp. Remember to place it in this position for mitring or your mitres will be in the wrong plane.

SHADOW BOX

A shallow display case for three-dimensional objects is made with two frames, an outer one holding the glass and an inner one holding the mounted object. The frame-making technique is exactly as described in the last chapter.

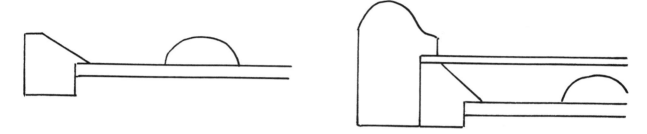

Fig. 53   Two stages in making a shadow box.

As with all framing operations start with the centre, i.e. the art, and work outwards. The object should be mounted as outlined in Chapter 3 and then an inner frame made to hold it (without glass). Then make your outer frame to take glass and this inner frame (as shown in Fig. 53).

The outer frame needs to be deeply rebated if there is to be no back projection. A large hockeystick moulding is often the answer. If you want to use a shallower moulding you can extend the rebate with added stripwood. This should be glued and pinned on before the mitres are cut so that it is sawn as a complete moulding. It is easier to handle in pre-cut lengths just a little longer than the required finished length. If the finish is to include a stain apply it to both moulding and rebate wood before you glue them together. Then, when dry, glue the stripwood to the base of the moulding and hold it with G-clamps (C-clamps) and extra wood as illustrated in Fig. 54. It should also be pinned for added holding power (from underneath) but make sure that these are not placed in the way of your mitres.

When assembling your shadow box fix first the mounted art into the inner frame and then the glass into the outer. The two can then be fitted together. The inner frame should slide in snugly; you should not need to force it, neither should it be able to move inside the outer frame. If there is any slight movement you can wedge in a sliver of

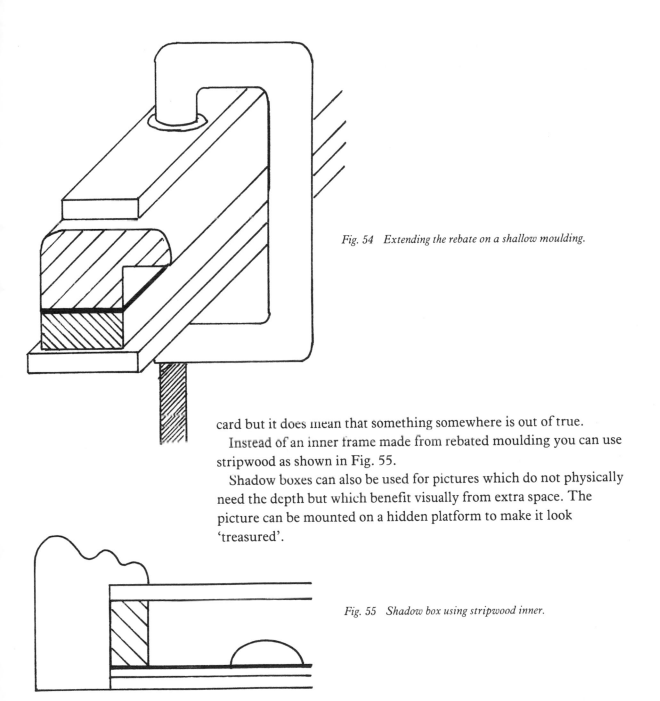

Fig. 54 *Extending the rebate on a shallow moulding.*

card but it does mean that something somewhere is out of true.

Instead of an inner frame made from rebated moulding you can use stripwood as shown in Fig. 55.

Shadow boxes can also be used for pictures which do not physically need the depth but which benefit visually from extra space. The picture can be mounted on a hidden platform to make it look 'treasured'.

Fig. 55 *Shadow box using stripwood inner.*

GLASS TRAP OR DOUBLE-SIDED FRAME

This is a free-standing frame with glass on both sides to display a two-sided document, a piece of lace perhaps, or simply two photos back to back. There are three ways in which it can be made.

1) Two moulding method: simply make two identical frames and glue them back to back with the art and two pieces of glass sandwiched inside as shown in Fig. 56a. This is aesthetically satisfactory in that the frame is truly reversible. It is necessary, however, to choose the moulding with care in order to get a double rebate depth that is exactly right for two pieces of glass and the enclosure; there is no opportunity for packing out excess space. If the rebate is a little too large you could opt for 3 mm glass on one or both sides to take it up.

2) A slightly cheaper version uses rebated moulding on the front and a mitred rectangle of plain stripwood on the back as shown in Fig. 56b. This is for art that has a definite 'front' but an occasional need to refer to the reverse.

3) The cheat's version uses the channel section sold amongst most ranges of builder's mouldings. Sizes may vary because they are not made to a fine tolerance but it should not be difficult to find a length that offers a snug fit to two pieces of glass and one of paper. It will be necessary to take your 'sandwich' to the shop for a fitting to be sure you are buying the right section. When making up the frame do not glue the bottom member at the same time as the others although it will of course be necessary to clamp it dry (see Fig. 56c). Pin the two top corners only and then slide the contents into this three-sided frame from the bottom. Glue in the fourth side and clamp again. When the glue has dried you could attempt to pin the corners in the normal fashion but the hammer blows could prove fatal. It is better to use small screws upwards from the base as described in the next paragraph.

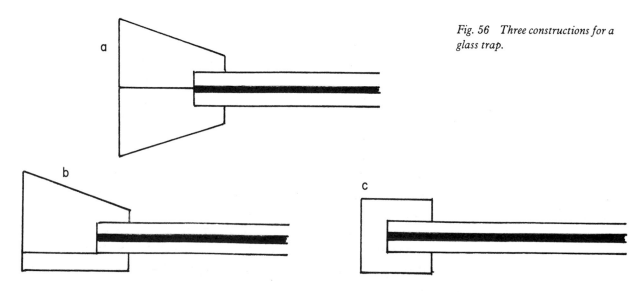

Fig. 56   Three constructions for a glass trap.

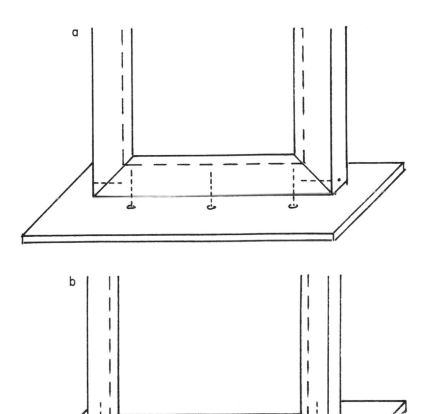

Fig. 57 Two ways of screwing the base to a glass trap.

Glass traps usually need some sort of base on which to stand firm and this can be a rectangle of wood as plain or fancy as you care to make it. It must be both glued and screwed from underneath into the base of the standing frame. If you have used a thick moulding small screws should not penetrate beyond the body of the moulding into the rebate (but keep away from the path of the nails in the mitres). See Fig. 57a. If however your moulding is small you will have to keep the screws at the ends and, in order to avoid collision with the mitre pins it is better to omit these altogether and use the screws to do both jobs. See Fig. 57b.

Glass traps tend, by the nature of their construction, to be permanently sealed units. There is no opportunity, unless you have been very ingenious, to open them and change or adjust the contents.

PASSE PARTOUT

This was the old-style, low-cost method of home framing, which has now gone out of fashion. It can only be used for small frames. Edge-smoothed glass and hardboard are sandwiched either side of the art and held in position with special non-stretch adhesive tape. It is first applied with lapped joints on the corners. These are subsequently mitred with a razor blade as illustrated. Unless the whole operation is carried out with 100 per cent precision the result looks a bit homespun.

Fig. 58 Mitring the taped corners on passe partout.

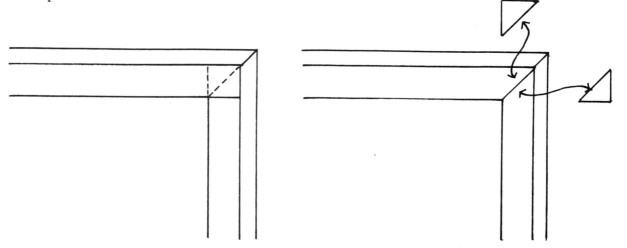

'NO-FRAME' METHODS

These systems have been largely responsible for the decline of passe partout because they are an easier option for the home framer who does not actually want to make a frame. They afford even less protection to the art than passe partout but are very popular for modern reproductions and photos, particularly for temporary exhibitions, on account of their low cost.

The picture, mounted or otherwise, is sandwiched between glass and hardboard. The hardboard must be substantial (at least 3 mm) because it supports the glass. If Emo or Swiss clips are used it must also provide a safe anchorage for the locking pin.

The glass may be 2 mm but 3 mm is more rigid and less likely to break. It is also easier for the glazier to burr the edges on the machine; the edges must be very well smoothed.

The sandwich is held together by one of the types of clip or bracket shown in Figs. 59 and 60. These systems are on sale in art and framing shops and some homecraft stores.

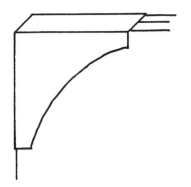

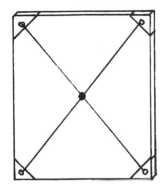

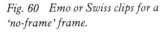

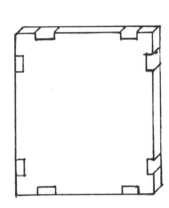

Fig. 59 Corner brackets and edge clips for a 'no-frame' frame.

Fig. 60 Emo or Swiss clips for a 'no-frame' frame.

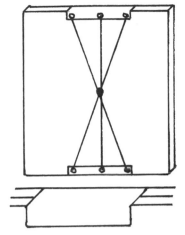

FRAMES FOR WORKS OF GREAT VALUE

It may be called archival, conservation or museum framing, but what it boils down to is a collection of rules for ensuring that the art has little or no opportunity for coming into contact with damaging substances. First and foremost of these is the acid present in wood and ordinary papers. The framing method is also designed to exclude all atmospheric threats.

1) Use acid-free board (as described in Chapter 3) both in front of and behind the artwork.
2) No pencil marks should be made on the board; pinpricks must suffice.
3) Cut surfaces of the board (such as the bevel edge) must be sealed with shellac.
4) No self-adhesive tape should be used anywhere. It is generally

assumed that if you lick it, it is safe. This is only partly true; water-based gum is safer but saliva is very acid, so damp the gum with distilled water. The carrier for the gum should be Japanese tissue – sometimes called rice paper although it comes from the mulberry tree – or linen tape.

5) Seal the rebate of the frame with shellac. Raw wood contact is a source of acid attack.

6) Tape the glass edges to the rebate before putting in the art; this is an extra anti-dust, anti-damp seal.

Lastly of course it goes without saying that you do not trim, paste down or modify the art in any way. Do not even fold the edges if it is really valuable. As well as this, make no constructional blunders in putting the frame together; there is no point in taping in the glass if you have a gapped mitre. In short, do everything to perfection! This perhaps explains why this section has been included in a chapter headed 'Variations'.

7 · GLASS

Picture glass can be bought cut to size from your local glass merchant. There is no price saving if you buy large sheets and cut your own unless you work in extremely large quantities. However, learning to cut your own is a worthwhile exercise because it enables you to reuse old glass from unwanted frames and to cut smaller pieces from broken or faulty sheets.

Picture glass is thinner than window glass, being 2 mm ($^1/_{16}$ in). Before metrication it was called 18 oz glass. Very occasionally you may come across thinner glass; if so take care of it because it is a fragile rarity. Obviously the thinner the glass between the eye and the picture, the less the refraction. However, if your picture is 1 metre or more in any direction you should consider 3 mm glass, particularly if the lip of the frame is narrow. 3 mm glass is less flexible and less inclined to bow under its own weight in the frame.

Non-reflective glass is roughly twice the price of clear picture glass. One side has a lightly stippled surface to diffuse the light falling onto it. This scattering of the light means that fine lines and colours tend to be dulled a little, and for this reason it is not generally used for good prints or watercolours. The slightly frosted appearance is not noticeable provided that the glass is close against the subject, but if it is used with a mount or fillet creating a space behind, its opacity becomes quite obvious and the picture appears fuzzy. The best application for this glass is perhaps on strongly-toned reproductions of oil paintings that might look inappropriate if obviously glazed.

Old glass is more likely to have bubbles or ripples in it if it was made by the rolling process that preceded the modern drawing and float processes. These flaws may not be too obvious in a picture full of colourful detail but they show up sharply if they fall against a mount or an area of solid colour. Old glass embrittles with age so take care when cutting it; it can shatter unpredictably.

Mirror glass is sold in 3 mm and 4 mm thickness. 3 mm is of a slightly lower optical quality because it is made by drawing upwards rather than by the float process. If you look at it closely edge-on you may be able to see slight ripples, but it is most unlikely that you would be able to detect any difference in normal use.

Glass merchants can re-silver old mirrors but the cost is more per square foot than the price of a new mirror. You might choose to do it perhaps for an unusually-shaped mirror with a nice bevelled edge but you should take advice if the mirror is likely to be of any value. Re-silvering genuine antique mirrors lowers their value.

Various glass substitutes are available through glass merchants and some homecraft superstores. Some are acrylic, others are polycarbonate or styrene. Most are more expensive than ordinary picture glass, although one non-reflective acrylic sheet is priced at about the same level.

These glass substitutes suffer from a number of disadvantages. They scratch easily and the cheaper ones can be difficult to find in large sheets without flaws. Some may go slightly yellow or cloudy in strong ultraviolet light. They are all difficult to cut. They are also more inclined to build up a static charge which attracts dust. However, it must be said in their favour that they are light, almost unbreakable and less inclined to collect condensation. Some of the more expensive ones actually protect the paper from sunlight deterioration by filtering harmful rays.

HOW TO CUT IT

Glass cutting should be done on a large, flat table cushioned with felt or an old blanket. Thick newspaper can suffice but it can be difficult to follow your markings against the background of the print. It is best to work alone because, until you are used to it, glass cutting can be a nerve-racking experience and you will not cut with concentration or confidence if, for example, you are keeping one eye open for the approach of small children.

Begin with small pieces (but not with dimensions of less than 50 mm or 2 in) and never attempt to cut a piece larger than your worktable or indeed any piece over which you cannot reach comfortably.

The glass must first be cleaned, partly to enable you to see imperfections and your own cutting marks but also because dirty glass is more liable to fracture. Avoid patent cleaning fluids because they tend to leave a filmy residue. A cotton cloth lightly damped with methylated spirit should take off grease marks but beware of too much spirit because that too can leave a slight mottling pattern. You can wash the sheet in warm water and detergent, rinse it, dry it and finally polish it with a squeezed out chamois leather. Try not to rub too vigorously or you will set up a static charge which will attract dust.

Old glass may be heavily marked with paint or varnish round the edges (the hallmark of the bodger who repaints frames without separating them from their contents). White spirit should deal with this. If any further stains remain try a brass cleaner or a vinegar (2 parts) and water (1 part) mixture. Cloudiness can sometimes be removed by soaking in ammonia and water.

Mirrors can be cleaned in the same way as ordinary glass. Flyspecks on old mirrors can be lifted with a solution of caustic soda (1 part) and water (20 parts). This is a ferocious mixture so wear rubber gloves and take care not to splash.

Use a good glass cutter; they are not expensive. For a novice the best sort is the type with a revolving wheel bearing six cutters as shown in Fig. 61. If you damage one with incorrect cutting you simply loosen the centre screw and rotate the next wheel into position. Keep the cutter standing in oil or spirit to prevent it rusting and also to help lubricate the cut. (This lubrication is not needed if you are using a diamond cutter.)

There are several ways of taking and marking your measurements. First it is as well to check that the sheet of glass you are using has right-angled corners and parallel sides. Then either:

1) measure the rebated size of your frame and deduct 3 mm from each length to allow for fit;
2) use the backing board as a template, provided that it is a good fit in the frame (this is a good idea if you have a frame that is slightly out of true);
3) place the corner of your glass into the top left-hand corner of the frame and mark the start of your cutting line for the top right-hand corner. Sight and mark the bottom corners. Remove the glass for cutting. This is also a better method than 1) for a frame that is slightly out of square.

A glazier will actually cut the glass while it is resting in the frame like this, but this is a practice to admire rather than to emulate until you are quite experienced.

Make your marks with a felt tip pen. Place your ruler or straightedge (preferably metal but a strip of wood will do) in position, taking into account the width of the cutter head, which means that the scoreline may come out about 3 mm to the right of the straightedge. If you think your ruler may slip, stick a strip of masking tape to its underside.

Hold your cutter like a pencil and begin to cut from the far edge of the glass (but do not let the wheel overhang it). Draw it towards you slowly but steadily with constant pressure and with confidence which, above all else, is the secret of successful glass cutting. There should be

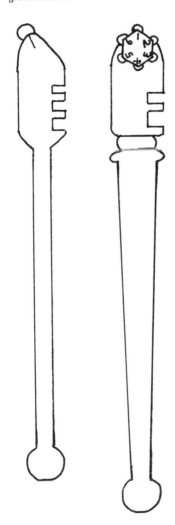

Fig. 61 Single and multi-wheel glass cutters.

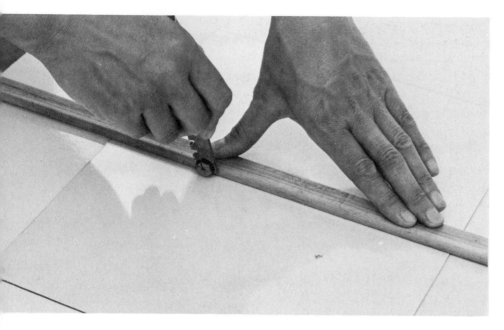

a gentle hiss but no crunching or crackling. Beware the natural tendency to ease up as the cutter nears your body which would cause a sloping curve in your break. Continue the cut to the bottom edge but do not run over it.

Turn the glass so that its bulk is supported on the table and the

Preparing to break the glass over the edge of the bench.

A clean break.

scoreline is about half an inch over (and parallel to) the edge. Turn yourself such that you can comfortably place your left hand on the supported glass and take the overlapping piece in your right. Sharp downward action with your right hand should snap the piece cleanly off.

Breaking the glass over the ruler.

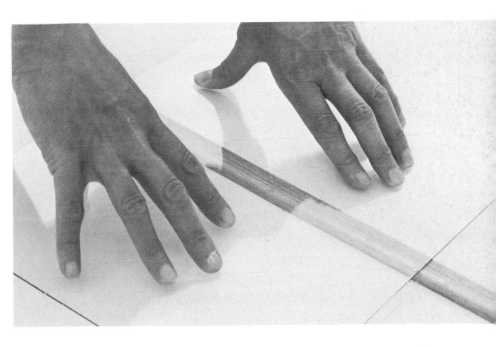

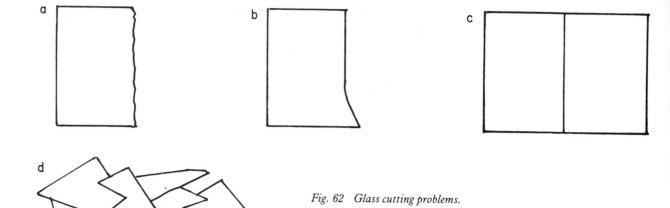

Fig. 62 Glass cutting problems.

If the glass is too large to handle comfortably like this, slide your straightedge under the glass, close to the scoreline, thus lifting one side of the glass slightly off the table. Press this side firmly for a clean snap. The professionals do it by taking the bottom edge in finger and thumb either side of the scoreline and flicking outwards.

The scoreline tends to 'heal' if this operation is not performed immediately after cutting because it is in fact a partially reversible molecular change in the scoreline that makes a clean break possible, not simply a cutting through.

If it all goes wrong (Fig. 62)

1) The glass breaks with a ragged edge (a): this is caused by uneven pressure or perhaps a worn cutter wheel. Take off the teeth with snub-nosed pliers or use the notched edge of your glass cutter. If the edge is still a bit rough, smooth it with an oilstone.

2) The break curves away at the bottom (b): this probably happened because you lightened the pressure as you got to the end of the cut. It may be possible to take off all or part of this curve with a second snap and then clean up the edge with pliers.

3) It does not break at all (c): this is most frustrating because the scoreline is clearly visible so the glass cannot be used for anything else. Try tapping on either side of the scoreline, from underneath, with your glass cutter. If it still will not break you must resist the temptation to cut again because it will not improve your chances and may damage the cutter wheel. One unorthodox remedy is to turn the glass over and begin to score along the back side of the line. The

pressure of doing this often achieves the fracture before you have got to the bottom.

4) The sheet shatters (d): bad luck – it may not have been your fault anyway because glass is very temperamental. If it had been stressed in some way before you started the cut a random fracture could easily result.

5) The glass is too big for the frame: tight glass is to be avoided so do

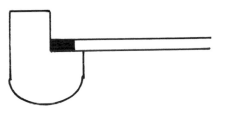
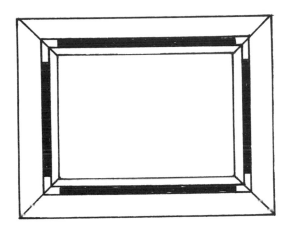
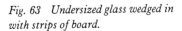

Fig. 63 Undersized glass wedged in with strips of board.

not try to force it in. It might seem secure this way but you will be stressing both the glass and the mitres. If the excess is very small you may be able to remove it with an oilstone or wet emery cloth. If this is insufficient you might consider paring away some of the wood from the inside of the rebate of the frame. This can be done with a utility knife or chisel. It is really only feasible for a short distance along one side, say, for a piece of glass that is slightly out of square. You will probably come to grief if you try to trim a few millimetres off the glass itself by cutting. It would be better to take both glass and frame down to your local glass merchant and ask him to do it for you. Do not be deceived by the ease with which he does it.

6) The glass is too small: not much can be done about this unless the deficit is very little. If your frame has a wide lip you can cut strips of card to fit around all four sides and wedge the glass in place (see Fig. 63) but it must be very secure. Do not rely on the final closing of the frame to hold it still. When you peer into the edges of the frame from the front you should not be able to see the reflected edges of the glass.

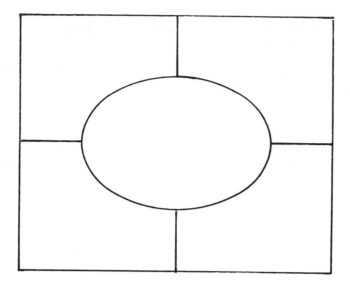

Fig. 64   Scoring the waste when cutting a glass oval.

Cutting acrylic sheet

In theory it is easy because the recommended method is to make repeated passes with a utility knife and steel rule, but in practice it is quite difficult to get a good clean break. Sawing is not advised unless a power saw with a carbide-tipped blade is used.

Ovals and circles

Normally you should not try to break along more than one cutting line at a time. However, in cutting ovals and circles without a proper jig it can help to split the waste as shown in Fig. 64. Start with a rectangle of glass whose sides exceed the axes of your figure by at least 50 mm (2 in). Use a template to score the oval on the middle. Then score lines out to the centre of each outer edge. Snap off each corner by hanging it over the edge of the table.

Edge smoothing

This is not necessary for glass going into a rebated frame because the edges will be hidden, but if you are cutting glass for a 'no-frame' frame you must have the edges smoothed. Glass merchants have a burring machine for this but you can do it with a wet emery cloth. Remember to do all eight faces.

8 · FINAL ASSEMBLY

Your artwork is mounted or laid down, your glass cut to size, your frame finished to perfection. All that remains is to marry these three components together successfully. The procedure might seem simple but blunders at this stage are particularly regrettable if you have taken the trouble to carry out all the earlier operations with care.

You need good light – preferably daylight – a clean work area and no sense of urgency. With a finished product in sight there may be a tendency to throw it together in haste for some deadline; this must be avoided.

Place the frame face down on a soft but firm and level surface. You do not want to mar the finished surface. Clean your glass and check once more that it lies comfortably in the frame. If it rocks a little there may be a blob of dried adhesive in one corner; it can be removed with a sharp blade. If your frame has not been made flat it will now be obvious. The weight of the glass, picture and backing may force it flat when they are fixed in, but this will mean stress on the corners. If the frame contents are lightweight and the moulding is heavy then the frame will 'win', as it were, and the result will be a small gap between the glass and rebate, through which dust, damp and insects will enter.

Next check the artwork for fit. If it is slightly too large you can of course consider trimming it, but remember to trim on all four sides to keep the margins uniform. If the mounted art is too small you may get away with packing the edges as described in the last chapter for undersized glass, but really you should consider remounting.

Now try art and glass together in the frame and view from the front to get an idea of the final effect. Any geometric defects in your mounting which have so far gone unnoticed will now show up in the symmetry of the frame, and this is your last chance to correct them.

BACKING MATERIALS

Your backing board may well have been cut already because it can serve as a handy template for testing the fit of the frame, size of glass etc without jeopardising the art itself.

Grey pulpboard is available from art shops and is ideal for small or medium-sized work. Make sure you get the thickest type available (3-4 mm). There are thinner versions which are not sufficiently rigid for frame backing. Corrugated board (as used for cartons) can also be used if it is clean and unbent, but in time the stripe pattern of the corrugations will transfer to the picture if it is not interleaved with white card. Corrugated board tends to be thicker and lighter than pulpboard and you may find that it protrudes from the back of the frame. Both pulpboard and corrugated board can be easily cut with a utility knife and steel rule (keep a scrap piece of pulpboard underneath the cutting area to prevent the blade from blunting too quickly on the work surface).

Hardboard (the thinnest type will suffice) is recommended for larger pictures. It is possible to cut it with a utility knife but it makes short work of blades. Sawing is better. You will need a general-purpose saw that does not have a ridge along the top of the blade (as does your mitre or tenon saw). Sand the edges well after sawing or you will introduce a lot of dust into your frame.

For really large pictures and mirrors plywood should be used as backing.

Oil canvases should not be backed with solid board because this would inhibit ventilation of the canvas and mould growth could result. They do, however, need to be protected from accidental 'poke-through' damage and this is best done with peg board which allows some airflow.

If you have a deeply rebated moulding that is only partly filled by the frame contents, you may wish to raise the level with some lightweight packing. You can use scrap pulpboard or even sheets of newspaper but these add considerably to the overall weight. Corrugated card is better (provided that it is not in direct contact with the picture) or polystyrene sheets (as used for ceiling tiles). You do not have to have one complete sheet because the backing board will provide rigidity.

GETTING IT ALL TOGETHER

The dummy runs are now over and you are confident that it will all fit and look right. Your glass should be clean but will probably be dusty. Try to avoid rubbing it too vigorously because this sets up a static charge and makes it attract dust even more. You may find that an anti-static record cleaning brush or cloth gets the specks off. Beware of making fresh fingerprints around the edge as you insert it into the frame.

A perfectionist will now seal the edges of the glass with very thin adhesive tape to prevent dust and moisture entering the frame from

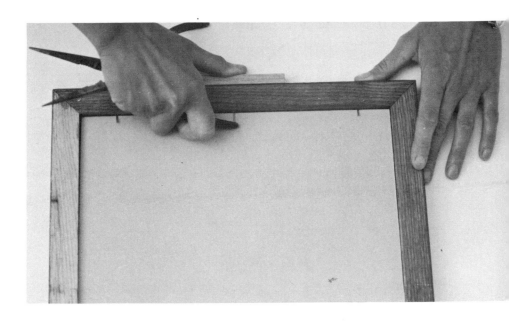

the front. It is not normal commercial practice.

At this stage you can now put in an inner frame or fillet if you are using either. If your picture is unmounted it is worth taking the trouble to cut thin (i.e. less than the width of the lip) strips of card to glue around the inside edges of the glass, thus lifting it off the art.

Now dust your artwork and examine it closely for clinging hairs, particles etc. When you are satisfied place it in the frame and insert the backing. If the picture is small enough to handle comfortably turn it over now and check from the front. At this stage you cannot check too often; if you rush into nailing and sealing the picture face down you will almost certainly find hairs, dust and other foreign bodies on display when you turn it over. The other hazard to watch for is slippage of the artwork. Unless the fit between picture and frame is perfect there will be a minute opportunity for the picture to lie crooked. This will be glaringly obvious from the front. The fault can be remedied of course, but it is very frustrating to pull out all your fixings and start again.

IRONMONGERY

There are several methods of fixing the frame contents in place. The cheapest and simplest is to drive brads or small veneer pins (i.e. a near-headless fixing) into preformed holes at about 75 mm (3 in) intervals around the rebate. They can be hammered gently into place with a

95

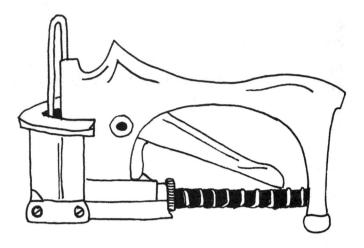

Fig. 65   Glaziers' gun.

flat-sided hammer, but a less risky method is to squeeze them in using the handles of a pair of pliers. Be careful, particularly if your moulding is narrow and of soft wood like virola or lauan, not to squeeze so hard that the point emerges through the back of the moulding. Until you have practised the technique it is advisable to protect the thumb of your left hand. Too much pressure at the wrong angle can cause the pin to jump over the edge and bury itself in your thumb.

Professional framers use a glazier's gun which fires triangular or diamond shaped points (Fig. 65). This is a very fast and efficient method and the fixture is flat and neat. It is well worth considering buying one of these guns if you intend to frame regularly. They are available from suppliers of picture framers' sundries or you may be able to locate a local supply through your glass merchant. The points come in 9 mm, 11 mm and 13 mm sizes; 13 mm triangles are suitable for almost all frames.

The gun is spring-powered and drives the sharp points with considerable force so keep it away from children. When firing into the frame make sure the other side of the moulding is braced against something solid to absorb the blow. Without such support the impact of each application can bow the frame member and strain, if not burst, the mitres at either end.

If your moulding has a shallow rebate, or if perhaps you have used a spacer, you may find that the frame is flush-filled, i.e. the backing is on a level with the underside of the moulding and you cannot get a fixture into the wall of the rebate. You can bevel your backing, that is to say cut a sloping V-shaped channel for a pin to be angled down into the rebate. It needs to be driven in sufficiently far for the head end not

to protrude above the backboard. Alternatively you can use screwturns
or turnbuttons.

Screwturns can be twisted by hand into preformed holes (made in
the underside of the frame) but it is easier to use a screwturn driver
designed for the purpose. Screwturns and drivers are hard to find in
homecraft shops but are available through the trade. (A bent veneer
pin carefully hammered into place – bend it before you hammer it –
does the same job but is not so firm or neat.)

Brass turnbuttons come in several sizes and are fixed with a small
screw into the underside of the moulding. They are readily available in
small packs from homecraft stores. If you want to change the contents
of your frame easily (e.g. a school photo which is to be annually
updated) they are an ideal fixture because as their name implies they
can be turned by hand if not screwed down too tightly. On small photo
frames they may be used in conjunction with brass kidney plates on

the top corners. Kidney plates are fixed with escutcheon pins (miniature brass nails); they look quite attractive on a standing frame whose back is in view, but they will not take much weight.

Spring clips (Fig. 67) can be used for flush-filled frames or where the contents of the frame are thicker than the depth of the rebate and stand proud of the back. They are firm fixtures but cannot be easily taped over to form a seal. They are, however, ideal for oil canvas stretchers as illustrated. Never nail a stretcher into a frame through its bars; this is sometimes done in cheap mass production but it makes it almost impossible to remove without damage.

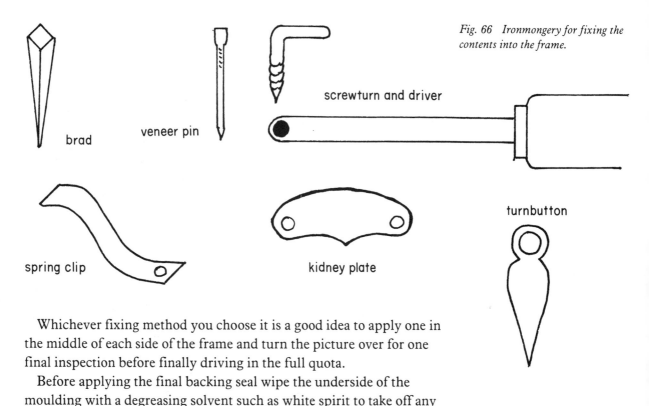

Fig. 66 *Ironmongery for fixing the contents into the frame.*

brad

veneer pin

screwturn and driver

spring clip

kidney plate

turnbutton

Whichever fixing method you choose it is a good idea to apply one in the middle of each side of the frame and turn the picture over for one final inspection before finally driving in the full quota.

Before applying the final backing seal wipe the underside of the moulding with a degreasing solvent such as white spirit to take off any polish smears or finger grease that may have accumulated during handling. Do not apply the seal until this is fully dry. Adhesive tape will only bond well to a surface that is clean, dry and dust-free.

The seal is usually made with 50 mm (2 in) wide tape. Gumstrip (brown paper with a dry lick-and-stick adhesive) was the traditional method, but it does not age well and nowadays many framers use masking tape which is more expensive but longer lasting. Avoid packaging tapes (made from a variety of plastic films) which last no time at all. Cut four lengths slightly in excess of each side and press

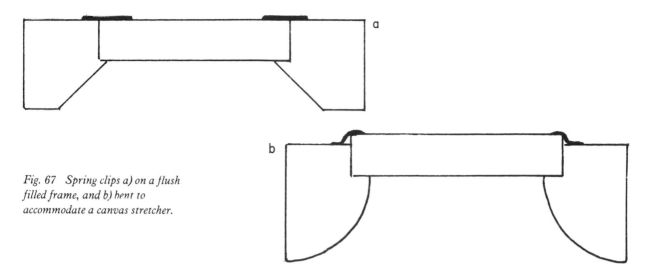

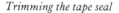

Fig. 67 *Spring clips a) on a flush filled frame, and b) bent to accommodate a canvas stretcher.*

them firmly into place. Then trim each corner to fit with a setsquare or ruler and a utility knife. Take care as you do this that the knife does not slip off the edge and score the finished back of the moulding; such scratches near the corners are the sure sign of a frame finished in a hurry. Rub the tape down hard and after a few minutes test each corner with your fingernail. If it lifts, you must rip the whole lot off and degrease more thoroughly.

The alternative to a tape seal is to glue a sheet of strong brown paper

Trimming the tape seal

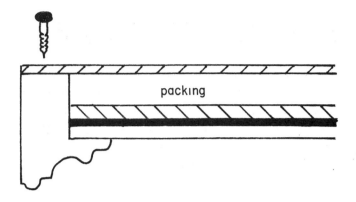

Fig. 68 Packing and reinforcing a weak frame.

over the entire backboard and moulding. This presents a much neater
finish if you are reusing old backing board that is marked or generally
grubby. The underside of the moulding must be degreased as for
taping and then, when dry, paste should be spread over the entire area.
Cut an oversized sheet of brown paper and damp it with a water spray
before laying it down onto the paste. This ensures a neat, taut fit
because it will shrink as it dries. When paste and paper are fully dry
the paper can be trimmed with a ruler and utility knife.

If you have doubts about the long term strength of your frame −
perhaps a narrow moulding being asked to carry a rather large area of
glass − you can take out an insurance at the backing stage by flush-
filling the frame with lightweight packing and screwing on a
hardboard backing cut to the full size of the frame. The hardboard
gives dimensional stability and takes some of the strain off the
moulding. It does, however, detract a little from the overall
appearance of the frame because it is marginally visible from the side.

9 · OLD FRAMES

The value of good quality old frames is now well recognised in the antique trade and you are not likely to find amazing bargains in a local junk shop. Genuine hand-carved wooden frames fetch a high price and their restoration is best left to experts. However, many lesser frames from the Victorian and Edwardian era can be picked up at a reasonable price, with or without contents, particularly if they are in poor condition. It is as well to be aware of the difference between those that are structurally sound but in need of surface attention and those whose mitres have loosened and will need to be remade. The latter will probably mean a reduction in the original size.

Taking old frames apart can be fascinating if you consider that you are opening up a very personal piece of handiwork which has been sealed for perhaps fifty years. Picture framers were far more numerous at the turn of the century (think of those picture-festooned walls in Victorian photographs) and usually advertised themselves boldly on the back of their work.

Your first task in dismantling an old frame with contents will be to tear off the brown paper sheet or tape which seals the back. It will probably have dried out and split already. Then, with long-nosed pliers, remove the sprigs or brads which secure the contents of the frame. A few decades ago it was customary to use thin sheets of birchwood as backing; in a large frame two or three might be necessary. On removing these you can lift out the artwork and the glass. You will probably be surprised at the dust, cobwebs, dead insects and general filth that have managed to penetrate the framer's defences.

Having emptied the frame check it thoroughly for woodworm, remembering that some holes in the rebate will be due to sprigs. If a gentle tap yields any fresh sawdust you definitely have a current problem. However, a very recent infestation may not show much visual evidence because the larvae have yet to emerge. If in any doubt treat the frame anyway and certainly keep all suspect frames in isolation until treatment is complete. Homecraft and household shops sell a variety of proprietary woodworm killers, some of which have a device for treating each individual hole. Since a picture frame is a relatively small area to treat there is no excuse for not doing it thoroughly.

Surface cleaning should be undertaken with care if you are uncertain as to the nature of the finish you are dealing with, assuming that you wish to clean it rather than replace it. Soap and water will remove surface dirt, but beware of slopping it around too liberally in the region of veneer, glued joints or plasterwork. White spirit or turpentine will take off wax polish and some forms of gold paint. Acetone is a fairly safe solvent cleaner to use on gilded surfaces.

Sometimes a stiff brush is needed to loosen stubborn deposits. Repeated applications of methylated spirit or a strong household soda solution will remove French polish that is no longer wanted; if on the other hand you want to cheer up a French polish that has lost its sheen it can be revived with equal parts of methylated spirit, linseed oil and vinegar rubbed on with a soft cloth.

Proprietary paint stripper can be used to take off old paint and some of the more stubborn types of varnish. There are now strippers which take off the old paint as a complete skin; these are particularly suited to the fine contours of mouldings. Follow the directions carefully, particularly with regard to skin protection, because all paint strippers contain powerful corrosives. A frame which has had several coats of paint may take several coats of stripper. No matter how painstaking your work you may find it impossible to get back to a surface sufficiently perfect for a stain and polish finish; in most cases you will have to repaint.

Maple or walnut frames are usually made from veneer, i.e. thin wafers of wood glued to a carcase frame of inferior wood. If sections of the veneer have lifted (due to drying out and shrinkage) it may be possible to replace them. Ideally you should use the proper cabinet-maker's glue but more likely you will settle for a modern equivalent. Having glued the sections down clean off all excess and weight them down for 24 hours. If the veneer is damaged, cut away a regular (i.e. square or rectangular) shaped section containing the damaged area and trace its outline on to replacement veneer. The best source for such scraps would be a traditional furniture maker or hardwood specialist. Craft kits tend to contain inferior wood that can be stained and polished to some sort of match but will not look as good as the original.

In renovating the surface of an old frame you need to be clear in your mind as to whether or not you wish to retain some of the antique character of the original finish. Much of the visual charm of old frames lies in their slightly worn appearance. It would be a shame, for example, to scrub off the patina of ages from a polished walnut frame merely in pursuit of modern cleanliness. Similarly a frame finished in genuine gold leaf may have a few blemishes with the passage of time but it would be disastrous to try and rectify them with a modern gilt substitute.

Not everything from the attic is a gem, however. You may come across hideous plasterwork which conceals quite a pleasant plain wood section underneath. To remove the plaster will take prolonged soaking – perhaps a week or more. This rules out the bath in most households so if you cannot achieve total immersion pack the frame with wet newspaper or sawdust and keep it freshly damp. If you cover it with plastic it will not dry out so fast but it may get a bit smelly. This soaking may also loosen the mitres.

You might, however, want to keep the plasterwork on a frame even though sections of it are missing. Broken moulding can be mended with car body filler, plaster of paris, gesso (a mixture of whiting and glue size) or a proprietary modelling material from an art shop. You can either build up an enlarged piece on the frame and then carve it down to meet the existing pattern or you can take a mould from an undamaged section with plasticine and use this to cast a replacement section. It can then be glued into place and painted to match the rest of the frame.

Old frames frequently have gapped mitres caused by the drying out of wood and adhesive. Movement in one mitre will frequently indicate that the others have been internally damaged by stress. The mitre joint is in fact one of the weakest in carpentry. Few frames that have done the rounds of salerooms and antique shops could really be described as structurally sound. If you are hoping to retain a wobbly frame in its existing size you can either dismantle the frame, hoping not to damage the ends, and reassemble without re-cutting or, if the weakness is not too pronouncd, use reinforcing plates of the type shown in Fig. 69 to hold the original construction together.

Opening up the mitres needs to be done with some care if you are

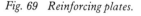
Fig. 69   Reinforcing plates.

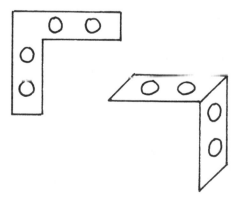

hoping to use each member untrimmed. Tap the nails out backwards as illustrated in Fig. 70 so that their heads do not tear through the wood. The old glue must be removed from each mitre face because new glue will not bond on top of old residues. If it is Scotch glue it should gradually dissolve in water. Solvent-based glues will probably have to be sanded off; take care not to sand away any wood thus altering the angle.

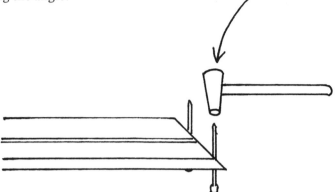

Fig. 70   Tap out old nails backwards.

If you are intending to strip or sand the face of the moulding, now is the time to do it rather than when the frame has been reassembled; your operations can be more vigorous without fear of loosening joints.

If it is not essential to retain the full size of the frame you will find it a lot easier to saw off a few millimetres at each end and begin with new mitres. The old ones may well have been inexact anyway.

If two diagonally opposing mitres are sound you need cut only two pairs of mitres to make a smaller frame as shown in Fig. 71. When siting your cuts make sure you are well clear of the concealed nails running through the corners. The hazard of this operation for the beginner is that it can be surprisingly difficult to achieve two identical halves when each is already glued into a right angle. Clamp your cut frame initially without glue and test the angle in each rebated corner with a setsquare before committing yourself to an adhesive bond.

Some old frames have been nailed so heavily through either side of the mitre that to try to open the ends would risk extensive damage to the ends of each member. The only recourse in such cases, if the size of the frame is not to be reduced, is to apply a set of reinforcing corner plates. They are not ideal as remedies. If applied only on the back of the frame they are not very strong; if applied on two faces they are visible. Fixing the plates is not without hazard. It can be difficult to locate and avoid the path of the nails in each corner. Secondly if you

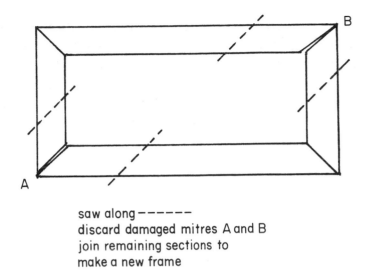

Fig. 71 Cutting down an old frame retaining two mitres.

saw along − − − − − −
discard damaged mitres A and B
join remaining sections to
make a new frame

have a frame of unusually hard wood such as oak, the little brass screws that come with the plates often shear off as you drive them in, leaving you with one fixing hole uselessly blocked and possibly no alternative position for the plate.

The contents of the frame may have less salvage value. The glass may be reusable when cleaned, but old glass tends to have more imperfections than modern glass and you may decide that these are unacceptable. If the flaws are not central you may be able to cut a smaller perfect piece out of it for another frame. Ironmongery should not be re-used unless clearly rust-free. If the mountboard is very unusual it could perhaps be cleaned with a soft eraser and light brushing but normally the mount and backing should be discarded.

When refitting the frame with new contents make new holes for the sprigs or brads. Try also to remove all traces of the old brown paper seal adhering to the back of the frame as these will prevent you from making a good seal with fresh tape.

10 · HOW AND WHERE TO HANG IT

Picture display seems to be on the increase again. The heyday of the last century when photographs of interiors show every wall space crammed with pictures has not quite returned, but the stark, bare wall fashions of the 1960s have given way to more ornamentation.

In choosing the site for a picture you have to consider functional as well as aesthetic factors, particularly if the picture is valuable.

1) Temperature and humidity changes militate against conservation. Continual shrinkage and expansion of wood, paper and adhesive eventually open up the frame to atmospheric attack. Kitchens and bathrooms therefore are not ideal locations for anything of permanent value.

2) Outside walls tend to accumulate condensation more than interior ones.

3) Radiators have a tendency to occupy prime wall space but they render the area above them unfit for pictures. The rising current of hot air rapidly dries out the frame and jet propels the invasion of dust and dirt.

4) Strong sunlight will fade mounts, watercolours and some inks; it also turns white paper yellow.

5) Watch out for the operational requirements of furniture. It is not a good idea to hang a picture where a carelessly opened chest lid or cupboard door could bang it. Detailed pictures need to be accessible for close perusal so do not hang them behind obstructions.

6) Plain, pale walls are the best background for most pictures. Strong colours and busy patterns deflect the eye away.

7) Security is another aspect. It is not a good idea to have valuable works in plain view to any casual caller at the door, nor to have them easily visible through a front window to anyone coming up the garden path.

Of course if you take all these admonitions to heart you will have empty walls, none fit to take a picture. An element of compromise is necessary to balance day-to-day enjoyment of pictures with their survival requirements. It is, however, as well to be aware of the hazards should you have something that you would like to hand on to your grandchildren in the same condition as it was when you first hung it.

Diffused light from the side is best for viewing pictures. A picture hung directly opposite a window will reflect glare and the outline of the window frame. Spotlights can be used to draw attention to a picture but they should be angled to reflect the light down to mid-body level rather than into the face. Galleries use shaded striplights fixed above the frame but these tend to look a little out of place in anything less than a baronial hall. Pictures which reflect too much light should be tilted forwards slightly from the top either by fixing a small length of wood behind the top or by moving the screw eyes further down the sides.

Pictures hung in damp areas will tend to collect condensation behind them, which can lead to mould growth. A small piece of wood or cork propping the picture slightly out from the wall allows air to flow more freely around it. This is also a good idea for oil canvases which need to 'breathe'.

GROUP HANGING

When hanging a pair of pictures aim for accuracy in the placement of your hooks; if you do make an error you may be able to compensate (vertically, at least) by adjusting the tension on the hanging wire. A plumb line and a tape measure will help you ensure that the hooks are level, provided that you live in a modern house whose rooms have right-angled corners. If you do not, a spirit level will be necessary. A makeshift one is shown in Fig. 72. (Another pair of hands becomes essential at this stage.)

Fig. 72   Makeshift spirit level.

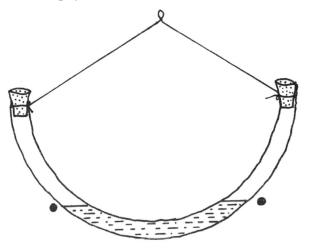

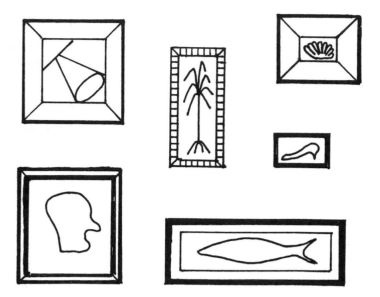

Fig. 73 *Group hanging by the 'lane' method.*

If the lines of your walls, shelves and window sills are already wildly out of true you may find it better to judge the levels of your two pictures by eye in context rather than adhere to some irrelevant geometric truth which, since optical references will be taken from the surroundings, will probably look wrong anyway.

A group of pictures of varying sizes needs to be spaced in accordance with some unity to look right; a haphazard arrangement rarely works. The most common principles are:

1) the 'lane' or constant space method (Fig. 73) in which, though the sizes of the pictures vary, the space between them remains the same;
2) tops in line (Fig. 74), for a linear arrangement;
3) bottoms in line (Fig. 75), for a linear arrangement;
4) middles in line (Fig. 76) which allows both vertical and horizontal expansion of the group.

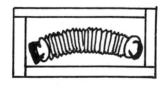

Fig. 74 *Group hanging, tops in line.*

108

Fig. 75 Group hanging, bottoms in line.

Fig. 76 Group hanging, middles in line.

Pictures on a stair wall should be lined up such that a line connecting their centres runs parallel to the incline of the stairs (Fig. 77).

Whichever method is used you need to work carefully with tape measure, plumb line and spirit level. Remember to measure and note the distance between the stretched hanging wire or cord and the top of the picture; also take into account that the point at which the nail enters the wall is a little higher than the point at which the picture rests on the hook. Unless you have a natural flair for precision in this sort of work it is not a bad idea to cut out, say, one quarter sized models of your pictures and plot the arrangement on squared paper.

HANGING FIXTURES

The most commonly used fixture is a pair of screw eyes driven into the sides of the frame at about one third of the way down from the top. Screw eyes (brass, steel, zinc or coppered) come in a wide range of sizes defined by the length of the shank in millimetres × the gauge. Choose a size compatible with the depth of wood that you are screwing into. It is very disheartening to ruin your frame at this late stage by driving in an oversized screw eye and have it burst through the front of the frame. (If this does happen, sand the hole with very fine paper, fill it and, when dry, touch it up with paintbox watercolour mixed to as close a match as you can get.) You will need to make a hole for the screw with a pointed tool such as a gimlet or birdcage awl. In softer

109

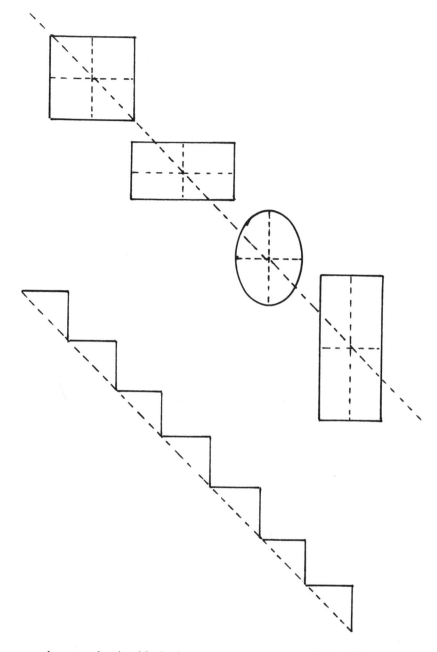

Fig. 77 Group hanging on a staircase.

woods an undersized hole does not matter too much but if you try to drive a brass screw eye into an undersized hole in oak the shank may break. (This tends to happen when the last screw eye is being fitted to a set of matching pictures, thus requiring all the others to be relocated!)

Some screw eyes are fitted with rings which help prevent abrasion of the cord or wire used for hanging, which would of course ultimately lead to failure. If you are worried about the durability of your screw eye fixing, use a second pair a little way above the first (see Fig. 79).

110

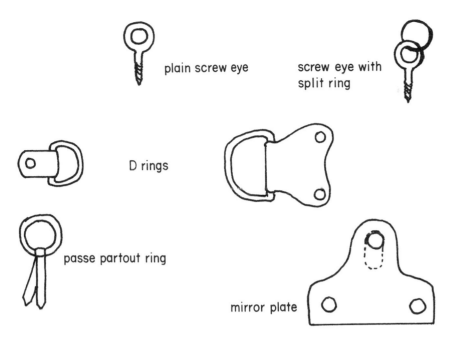

Fig. 78 Ironmongery for hanging.

plain screw eye

screw eye with
split ring

D rings

passe partout ring

mirror plate

These will act as a safety stop should the anchor screw eye pull out and with luck you should notice the picture hanging askew before it finally comes crashing down.

A more substantial fitting is the D ring. These are used for small mirrors and larger pictures. They protrude less behind the frame (and are for that reason sometimes specified for entries to art exhibitions) and thus allow it to lie flatter against the wall. D rings come in two sizes – with either single or double screw fixing – usually in nickel

Fig. 79 Use of twin screw eyes.

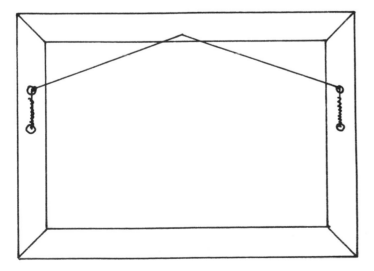

steel with round-head no. 4 screws, ⅜ in long. Check before use that you have that depth of wood in your moulding.

Fig. 80 Wiring screw eyes.

Passe partout rings are a lightweight hanging device for use where there is no wooden surround into which to fix a screw. They are rings with a split metal pin which is pushed through a slit in the backboard and splayed open to hold on the reverse. This fixture needs to be installed before the frame and its contents are assembled and sealed.

Mirror plates are the strongest wall fixing. They are available in brass in a variety of sizes in ¼ in intervals from 1 in to 2½ in height. They have two base holes and wood screws for fixing on to the back of the frame and one hole for the wall fixing. This may be round or slotted, the latter being for mirrors which you wish to take down without undoing the wall fixing. Although designed for mirrors they can be used for any picture where it is desired to hang flush against the wall (sometimes appropriate for a small picture in a wide moulding) or for security reasons in pubs, clubs and hotels where the clientèle are not trusted. The upper part of the plate protrudes visibly above the frame but it can be recessed into the wall and papered or plastered over if considered unsightly. Rawlplugs are necessary for secure fixing to walls and, unless the picture is lightweight, it is better to replace the screws provided in the retail pack with more substantial ones.

Flush display also looks better for block-mounted prints. In this case drill a small hole a few millimetres deep (take care not to burst through the front) near the top of the back in the exact centre. Marry this with a nail driven into the wall. You can use the same method with a lightweight picture (e.g. unglazed canvas) in a thick moulding if it is not too large. Two such fixings increase the security of the hold but call for great accuracy in placement of the holes and nails because there is no scope for adjustment.

The backs of pictures can be strung with cord or picture wire (not garden wire) of the stranded brass variety. Cord can be cotton, which rots, or nylon, which stretches. Both discolour with age. In general wire is to be preferred, although it can slip disastrously if not firmly moored. Wind it twice around the screw eye or D ring and allow at least a 50 mm (2 in) tail to twist along the length (see Fig. 80). Never pull it tight across the back; this will drag on the screw eyes. It is better to allow as much slack as is compatible with the height of the picture without uncovering the wall hook when it is hung.

Chain is the heavyweight solution for big mirrors and pictures. It is also used in conjunction with picture rails, because it is more visually acceptable than cord or wire.

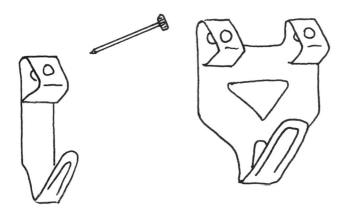

Fig. 81 Single and double wall hooks.

Proper picture wall hooks are much better than nails for wall fixing. There is less strain acting on the fixture and they are not so likely to wear through the hanging cord or wire. They also make the picture less prone to tilting on one side. Use two for heavy pictures. Single nails are permissible only for the most lightweight pictures or for flush hanging as described earlier.

If you are nailing your picture hook into plaster of doubtful quality stick a small square of adhesive tape over the site before driving it in. This holds crumbly plaster in place.

All the ironmongery described above can be bought in packs of small quantities from homecraft superstores but it is, of course, a lot cheaper to buy in bulk from a trade supplier.

113

11 · GOING PROFESSIONAL

Once you have achieved a demonstrable standard of attainment you will suddenly find yourself in great demand from friends. They tend not to emphasise that they see you as a cost-saving facility; the story generally goes more along the lines of 'My husband is always promising to frame it for me but he never seems to have the time'. You, by implication, have. When your delight at this new-found popularity begins to fade it is time to think about it as a source of income.

There is an awkward halfway stage when you are uncertain about how much to charge, since your first customers will tend to be friends. There comes a point when you have to become fairly hard-nosed and announce that you are now in business, albeit in your spare time, and that your services are no longer free. You will of course probably keep a close circle of friends and family for whom you frame at cost, but try not to let embarrassment widen this circle further than you intend, or you will never build up a body of full price paying customers.

When researching local competition you will probably be slightly alarmed to find that there are more framing services than you had realised. Apart from obvious well advertised professional framers, a number of other shops may be offering a framing service as a half-hearted sideline. Check out their prices by toting round a couple of pictures and asking for quotes with and without mounts. In particular try to discover where their service falls short. Is there a long delay in getting work finished? Does the price cover everything or does it get bumped up by extras such as hanging fixtures? Is the person who accepts work over the counter knowledgeable about the work or simply a sales assistant? Do you sense a general disinclination to take on work that calls for something other than a standard mount and frame? These are all areas in which you as a small framer could outpoint an established business. Another benefit that you might be in a position to offer is collection and delivery (but remember to incorporate such costs into your prices). Few framers offer a delivery service; virtually none will call to allow the customer to see samples in the context in which the picture is to hang. You are also more likely to secure the order if you have taken the trouble to come to the customer.

To help in your presentation you will of course need a portable set of samples. Make up mitred corner pieces of approximately 200 mm (7 in) from all your mouldings and mount corners in a span of widths (38 to 75 mm). Your pack must also include a measuring tape or folding ruler, pencil and paper and an order book with carbon because some customers will expect to be given a receipt for handing over their property, plus written confirmation of the quoted price. It is also handy to carry two small squares of glass – one clear and one non-reflective – because many customers think that they might want non-reflective glass without being too sure of what it looks like. Unfortunately such samples frequently come to grief in a sample bag so make sure they are well wrapped.

Arriving at a consistent set of charges is not easy because of the infinite number of variables involved in the work. You could spend long hours calculating a standard price table to cover all the likely permutations of size, moulding type, finish, type of glass etc, and the next customer to arrive will set it at nought by wanting an additional inner frame, or a spacer, or a fabric covering on the mount or non-reflective glass. Your pricing needs to be fairly flexible to take into account materials supplied by the customer, e.g. you may reframe a picture whose glass is still reusable. It is better therefore to keep a notebook of the prices you are currently paying for all your materials and cost each job on the basis of material input plus estimated work time at whatever rate you feel entitled to charge. You may choose to cut this price to meet competition or oblige a friend but you then do so knowingly. You should of course keep a basic record of incomings and outgoings not simply for your own awareness but also in case you are called to account by the taxman.

You should also consider taking professional advice on the subject of insurance. You will be handling and storing other people's property and you run unavoidable risks of theft or damage that would probably not be covered by a normal domestic or auto policy. It is a good idea to ask customers to estimate the value of pictures that they are entrusting to you, and if you feel that you would prefer not to have the responsibility of holding it then take measurements and cut a sheet of card to meet the exact size (verify it on the spot in the customer's presence) and the customer can then take the valuable picture home. There will of course be a slight delay on collection when the customer has to wait while you fit the actual picture into the frame that has been made for the dummy card, but this is better than finding yourself the subject of an enormous claim.

Framing for cash at commercial prices means framing to commercial standards. This means that you should consider investing in some professional equipment. The two most basic items over and above the tools you have already acquired for hobby framing are some form of powered saw and a bench mount cutter. Even if your hand sawing and hand mount cutting have reached an unusual standard of excellence the method will be too time consuming when you start to build up a volume of work, and you will not be able to charge a fair return for your time without pricing yourself out of business.

These items of equipment represent a fairly major investment (although not excessive by comparison with what, say, a keen amateur photographer might spend in pursuit of his hobby). Suppliers are listed in the Appendix but you will want to see the equipment demonstrated. In the UK the best opportunity for this is at the Spring Fair which is held each February at the National Exhibition Centre in Birmingham. This is a vast exhibition lasting several days and covering a variety of trades from hardware to greetings cards. It usually has a good turnout of picture frame suppliers, not only of equipment but also mouldings, mountboard, ironmongery and sundries. It is well worth attending if you have serious commercial framing ambitions.

In the USA a nationwide exhibition of picture framing suppliers is included in the annual Chicago Hardware Fair. Additional trade events are organised by the Professional Picture Framers' Association whose address is given in the Appendix.

Some sort of business card is a worthwhile early investment. Even if you only have a handful of customers it establishes your professional credibility with suppliers and is often the passport to a trade discount. If you choose a postcard size with a brief statement of your services it can double as an advertisement on noticeboards. You will also need either printed labels or a rubber stamp with which to identify your work on the back. Be sure that this includes some statement to the effect of 'framed by . . .' so that you do not appear to be claiming authorship of the art itself.

Some of these measures may seem excessive, not to say expensive, when you are framing perhaps only one or two pictures a week. They nonetheless help to create an aura of professionalism which will serve you in good stead as business increases. Friends will find your pricing policy more acceptable and new customers will be drawn more readily to an enterprise that smacks of serious commercial intent. If you are so successful in this respect that the town beats a path to your door you may of course eventually arouse the interest of telephone and rating authorities who might feel inclined to reassess you as a business rather than a private customer. Unwelcome though this may be it does signify successful business development. It should, however, not arise as a problem if you wish to keep the operation at the level of a spare time paying hobby.

When the framing needs of your friends and family have been satisfied you will want to broadcast information about your services more widely. Check out everywhere in town where you can display your postcards at low cost or even for free. Arts centres, craft workshops, libraries, club noticeboards and many shops serving health or self-sufficiency type products, plus of course the ubiquitous corner newsagent display board are likely targets. Always carry a few cards around with you and be quite shameless about dropping them accidentally on purpose in environments where prospective custom gathers.

Advertisements in publications lead you a notch or two up the cost scale. Local magazines and papers are worth exploring; many offer low-cost advertising space. You will know that you are not wasting your money on readers beyond your geographical scope. Your business will come from within a radius of ten miles (give or take a few exceptions) and it is pointless to pay for informing people outside this area.

A good opportunity for promoting your wares in person is at local craft shows. These may vary from the 'Craft Tent' at a big agricultural show to a small charity event. You need to be fairly selective about these if you do not want to waste a lot of time. Your purpose will be to make a profit on the day's costs by selling ready-made goods − framed mirrors, photo frames, small framed pictures − and to advertise your 'bespoke' service. Since the unit cost of even the smallest photo frame can exceed the unit cost of many other types of craftwork you can too easily find yourself surrounded by stalls selling items at a fraction of the price of yours. No matter how much good value you are offering it is a bad pitch. Customers will be thinking in terms of small change if that is the general pricing tone and will shy away from your higher quality merchandise. Unless you are prepared to risk a wasted day (not to mention the stall fee) it is wise to visit such fairs on reconnaissance and see what sort of customers they attract, and then approach the organiser with a view to booking. It is of course sensible to stay within your business catchment area unless you have decided to major on the sales of ready-made frames.

Your pitch fee normally covers a table, chair and possibly a power point. The rest is up to you. Find out the size of the table in advance so that you can design and mock up an effective display; do not rely on last minute inspiration when you arrive on the day. If you do not want to go to the extent of building tiered racking, collect stout empty cardboard boxes and cut them down into supports. It is essential to have your frames − whatever their contents − propped up. A sea of frames lying flat on the table will not stop any customer in his or her tracks. A tiered display will also hold more. Cover the table with a cloth and spray paint your cartons and boxes to match.

Your ready-made wares could include mirrors to show off your more decorative and eye-catching mouldings, some photo frames in standard sizes, and some framed pictures. If you are uncertain of your market you will not want to risk investment in art simply for the sake of filling frames, so plump for the bottom end of the market and look for high quality greetings cards. Judging adult taste can be difficult, but children are easier and you can settle for nursery pictures which sell well, particularly at Christmas. Many card series now reproduce illustrations from children's classics which are popular.

Your stall should leave room for a sample board to indicate the bespoke side of your business and provide a topic for customers' casual enquiries. The simplest method is to fasten small squares of hook and loop fasteners on to your sample corners and your display board. If you use the hook halves on the samples you can then cover the board with a bouclé-type fabric to which the hooks adhere and thus have scope to change your sample arrangement around.

Have your price and order book to hand in case customers want to place a definite order. It is quite reasonable to ask for a deposit in such cases, particularly if the customer lives some distance away and you are not offering delivery. Deposits must be receipted. All your ready-made frames should be price-marked. You may perhaps have priced them low because they have been made from scrap odds and ends of moulding, but consider that some customers may take a liking to one and ask for two more to match. In such cases you need to have decided whether or not you can produce more to the same price. Some customers want to know what you would charge for bespoke framing and this can be difficult if you do not operate a formal price list. If the customer does not have a specific example in mind it is useful to have worked out in advance a selection of typical hypothetical job prices to quote. If a customer asks you to quote for an unseen picture saying vaguely 'about this size' make it clear that you are quoting for what you understand to be a specific size. People are notoriously unreliable in remembering dimensions and you could find yourself stuck with a low quote for a picture that turns out to be larger than you had understood it to be.

You will also need a good stock of business cards. Scatter about half a dozen on each front corner of your display table and keep them replenished. Fewer than four makes people reluctant to take one, thinking they might cause you to run out; too many looks profligate. A neatly arranged display of cards will remain untouched so make it casual. The fruits of this card distribution may come many months or even years later. Information about picture framers is something that people tuck away for future reference.

It goes without saying, of course, that you should be ready to engage passing customers in conversation without hovering in a predatory fashion over anyone who looks as though they might be stopped. Even if business is slack you should resist the temptation to sit down and open a novel. It is a good idea to have some occupation, such as polishing frames, which engages your hands but does not discourage people from interrupting you.

If you live well off the beaten track and cannot collect and deliver work you could think about selling through an existing retail outlet. If you are unknown you could start by approaching local gift and craft shops with framed mirrors and photo frames. Some shops may be prepared to accept them on a sale-or-return basis, or to sell them on your behalf and take a commission, but open negotiations for an outright sale and fall back on this only if the manager or proprietor is less than enthusiastic. If they go well you can then suggest that a bespoke service be initiated whereby you supply samples and point-of-sale material (this must be professionally produced) and undertake to collect and deliver regularly. Shop staff cannot of course operate your costing system so you will need to standardise your prices into a simple table based on common sizes and types. The shop will then add on a sales commission. You should also agree on a commission procedure for customers with whom you have to deal direct because their requirements are specialised but whose initial enquiry came through the shop.

APPENDIX
TOOLS, MATERIALS
& SUPPLIERS

The following is a list of framing requirements readily available from retail outlets. It is not an exhaustive catalogue of every item mentioned in the book but a basic starter kit. Trade sources for bulk supply and more specialised items are listed overleaf.

tenon or fine back saw
mitre block
G-clamps (C-clamps)
mitre clamp
awl
nailset
tack hammer
pincers
pliers
utility knife
glass cutter
straightedge
T-square
setsquare
steel rule
moulding

mountboard (matboard)
backboard
glass
panel and veneer pins
woodworking adhesive
masking tape
woodstain
sandpaper (several grades)
steel wool
filler
paint and varnish
French polish
wax polish
methylated spirit
white spirit
spray adhesive

UK SUPPLIERS

Lion Picture Framing Supplies
6 Mott Street
Birmingham B19 3HD
021 233 3073
(also stockists in Newcastle-upon-Tyne and Salisbury)

Distributor of mouldings, equipment, mountboard and all sundries

Ashworth & Thompson Ltd Lillington Road Bulwell	Manufacturer and importer of prefinished and raw timber mouldings in ramin, oak and pine.
Nottingham NG6 8HJ 0602 278504/5 (also showrooms in London & Dublin)	Also ironmongery, equipment and backing boards.
Framers Equipment Ltd Sutton Road Rochford Essex 0702 547121	Specialised tools and equipment (part of Magnolia Group – see below).
Magnolia Mouldings Ltd 145 Stoke Newington Church Street London N16 0UH 01 249 6961	Mouldings and equipment. No direct trade with individuals but telephone for local stockist. Cash and carry warehouse.
Frank B Scragg & Co. Ltd 68 Vittoria Street Birmingham B1 3PB	Ironmongery.
Arquati UK Ltd 2 Wolseley Road Kempston Bedford MK42 7AY 0234 857488	Mountboard and cutters, prefinished mouldings. Telephone for nearest stockist.
Lawrence & Aitken Ltd Albion Works Kimberley Road London NW6 7SL 01 624 8135	Wide range of mountboards especially acid-free museum board. No direct trade with individuals but telephone for local stockist.
J Fisher & Son 21 Bevenden Street East Road London N1 01 253 8655	Specialises in raw timber mouldings 3/8 to 3 in wide in pine, oak, ramin, mahogany, obeche. Also prefinished range.

D & J Simons & Sons Ltd
122 – 8 Hackney Road
London E2
01 739 3744/8

Prefinished and raw timber (ramin) mouldings. Embossed (carved) mouldings without rebates. Ironmongery & accessories.

Iris Mouldings Ltd
Platts Common Industrial Estate
Barnsley
Yorks S74 9SA
0226 744717

Prefinished mouldings.

H Burbidge & Sons Ltd
Whittington Road
Oswestry
Shropshire
0691 5131

Raw timber mouldings in ramin, oak, red cedar and utile. No direct trade with individuals but telephone for nearest stockist.

Other Useful Addresses

Fine Art Trade Guild
192 Ebury Street
London SW1
01 730 3220

Trade Association of manufacturers.

Framing & Art Buyers World
(12 issues p.a.)
83-5 Bridge Road
East Molesey
Surrey KT8 9HH

Picture framing training is offered by:

Sackville School of Framing
418 Brighton Road
South Croydon
Surrey CR2 6AG
01-681 1448

Origin Gallery (Croydon) Ltd
Ridges Yard
107 Waddon New Road
Croydon, Surrey
01-686 7462

Tim Elkington
Hill House
Little Rissington
Cheltenham
Glos GL54 2NB
0451 20426

Magnolia Group (Mouldings) plc
145 Stoke Newington Road
London N16 0UH
01-249 6961

USA SUPPLIERS

Picture Framing Equipment Inc. — Manufacturer and distributor
5836 North Commerce Plaza — of wide range of equipment
PO Box 10942 — and materials. Also runs
Jackson — Training Centre offering
Mississippi 39209 — 5 day beginners' courses.

Northwestern Moulding — Mouldings.
   & Picture Framing Co.
113 Washington Avenue North
Minneapolis

Melvin Picture Frame Co. Inc. — Mouldings.
20 T Marbledale Road
Tuckahoe
New York

Tower Picture Frame Co. — Mouldings.
2640 River Avenue
Rosemead
California 91770

Frame Square Industries   Equipment.
PO Box 569
Monroe
North Carolina 28110

Pistorius Machine Co. Inc.   Equipment.
1785 Express Drive North
Hauppage
New York 11787

Larson Picture Frame & Moulding
    Co. Inc.
422 T 3rd Street
PO Box 626
Ashland
Wisconsin

Supreme Frame & Moulding
1528 W Armitage
Chicago
Illinois 60622

Framers Supply Co. Inc.
2621 S 4th Street
Louisville
Kentucky 40228

Art Materials, Frames &
    Mouldings Co. Inc.
1205 Putnam
PO Box 5272

Huntsville
Alaska 35805

Frame Crafters Moulding &
    Supply
900 Central Avenue
Albany
New York 12206

Carolina Framing Supplies
PO Box 241106
Charlotte
North Carolina 28224

Arquati Inc.
3308 Garden Rock Brook Drive
Dallas
Texas 75234

Greco Frame & Supply Co. Inc.
3813 S Purdue
Oklahoma City
Oklahoma 73179

Other Useful Addresses

Professional Picture Framers'
    Association
4305 Sarellen Road
Richmond
Virginia 23231

Decor magazine (13 issues p.a.)
408 Olive Street
St Louis
Missouri 63102

AUSTRALIAN SUPPLIERS
J. Kosnar Pty Ltd
PO Box 264
Niddrie
Victoria 3042

G. and H. Partos Pty Ltd
337 Brunswick Road
Brunswick
Victoria 3056

Ronad Morris Mouldings Pty Ltd
138 Bonds Road
Riverwood
New South Wales 2210

Juhl Pacific Australia
CRN Clay and Reynolds STS
Balmain
New South Wales 2041

SOUTH AFRICAN SUPPLIERS
Design Products
Carey Street
Wynberg Ext. 1

Johannesburg Mouldings
Refinery Road
Driehoek
Germiston
PO Box 4191
Germiston South 1411

Supreme Mouldings (Pty) Ltd
1198 Beitel Road
Robertville
Florida
PO Box 214
Maraisburg 1700

Maree's Mouldings (Pty) Ltd
6 Currey Street
Doornfontein
Johannesburg
PO Box 15679
Doornfontein 2028

Sunshine Graphics
Shop USI
Eastgate
Bradford Road
Bedfordview 2008

INDEX

Figures in italics refer to page numbers of illustrations.